GO FOR A WALK. READ MORE BOOKS. CALL YOUR PARENTS. TAKE A REAL LUNCH BREAK. TURN YOUR PHONE OFF. EAT SOME ICE CREAM.

Laura Ann Creative, '20 Social Distancing Quotes', countryliving.com

WE'RE ALL BORN NAKED THE REST IS TECH.

Transformella Malor (Johannes Paul Raether), art&digitalculture/transmediale

HELP YOUR SELF!

HELP YOUR SELF!

The Rise of Self-Design

MIEKE GERRITZEN

Valiz, Amsterdam

The ultimate problem of design concerns not how I design the world outside, but how I design myself — or, rather, how I deal with the way in which the world designs me.

Boris Groys, 'Self-Design and Aesthetic Responsibility', www.eflux.com

FOR MY SELF

CONTENTS

After Supermarket Lady (1969-1970) by Duane Hanson

THE RISE OF SELF-DESIGN

We recognize 21st-century western mankind as not only well-dressed and well-groomed, but also as a species that cares about its inner life. We delve into the plethora of spiritual apps and self-help books that may make our lives more pleasant or even change them. Now that western mankind has more free time because robots do all the work and more time is spent at home or working from home, there is room for reflection and contemplation. The time has come to strike a balance between body and mind.

Who are you, who would you like to be, and what should you do to get there? We are constantly under pressure to lead a perfect life. The media hold up a mirror in which we lead a life in which we are rich, beautiful, happy, and successful. There was a time when our identity was defined by our neighbourhood, our family, and our friends, but nowadays we are supposed to write our own success story on social media platforms.

From spoons to entire cities, we are designing the world. We already have product design, interior design, graphic design, interaction design, and fashion design. And now there is also self-design. *Help Your Self!* introduces the notion of self-design because as a self-designer you have an extremely important assignment. Designing yourself is a personal challenge, but most of all a responsible task. How you position, profile, and manifest yourself in society not only determines your own happiness and well-being, but also that of your environment.

Most people have some idea of what self-design may be. We design our own identity, our own image, and we present ourselves as we like to be seen. The various ingenious methods and ideas to create a better version of ourselves — dieting to achieve the perfect body, converting our talents into a successful company, or find bliss in a new love — are regarded as new forms of creativity, or Self-Design.

Help Your Self! lets you surf on paper. *Help Your Self!* introduces you to the many aspects of self-design, ranging from developing your identity to designing your own death. It is a picture book that asks questions about how you want to do things or what you think of them. *Help Your Self!* is a book about man's pliability, about you as an individual in society, about how you shape yourself into the person you want to be. It is not scientific or all-encompassing, but it is full of knowledge and ideas about how you can create yourself. Although there are many things to fill out, the book is not intended as a self-help book nor is it an answer to the self-help industry, which by now in its vastness has become a real economic factor.

Help Your Self! reflects on the society in which you live. It looks gay enough but the book also shows you where the dangers lie. Visions of the future or how you may change or improve yourself have been around for centuries and so has the collecting of interesting facts, ideas, and thoughts. Even before there were encyclopaedias and dictionaries, there already were — soon after the invention of printing around 1450 — books of quotes. The urge to collect information is still in full swing and was given an enormous boost by the advent of the Internet.

Help Your Self! is an inspirational book to design your perfect self and it shows you how to make a start. At the same time, it reflects on the self-help industry is a relatively new phenomenon. Hopefully this is all of some use to you.
Help Your Self!

Science tells us who we are. But who we want to *be*, is a matter of culture. Of imagination. Of the humanities. They will become increasingly important when it comes to dealing with the ethical issues of major technological changes. The consequences of genetic interventions in human beings. More and more we are able to make man. But *how* shall we make him?

Bas Heijne, 'Deze vraag kan en wil de wetenschap niet beantwoorden', brainwash.nl

DASEIN IS
DESIGN

YOU ARE ALREADY HERE

You have a name and you live in a house, in a town or village. You are unique. There is only one like you, with your body, your smell, taste, glance, manner of laughing, speaking, doing, everything. Who you have become is based on a concurrence of circumstances, which you have combined with your own choices.

Because you are already here, this means that you are able to read this book about makeable mankind. Because both physically and mentally you can further design, change, and improve yourself with the aid of more and more technology and information. This is Self-Design.

Nowadays, people who are not even born yet can already be improved or adapted at the microscopic level by testing and manipulating genes or by applying stem cell and nanotechnology. But we won't go into that, since this book is for you and you are already here.

What do you do to be interesting and likeable to others? What do you want to look like, and for whom? How do you arrange your surroundings? What would you like to do most of all with the hours in a day, the days in a week, the weeks in a year? Are your ideas about that even your own ideas? And are your desires truly your own desires? Or are they just images from the media you strive to achieve? That's what we will be looking into. That's what we will be questioning and that's what we'll be giving you ideas about. You are already here. But who are you and who would you really want to be?

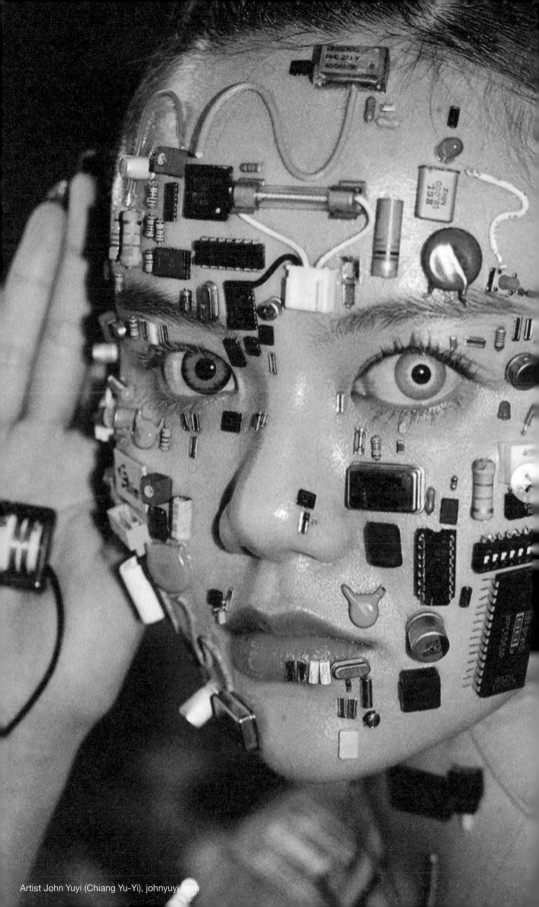

MANKIND IS A WORK OF ART

There was a time when we were part of nature, but since we began to see ourselves as individuals, we are compelled to be the creative creator of ourselves. We have given ourselves the immensely complex task of working on ourselves to obtain the desired result. This is both a philosophical and an artistic mission, as it concerns both the message and the packaging.

Today, everyone is subjected to an aesthetic evaluation — everyone is required to take aesthetic responsibility for his or her appearance in the world, for his or her self-design. Boris Groys, www.eflux.com

In politics this Self-Design has been around for ages. Barack Obama is a recent example. As President he not only concerned himself with every sentence in his speeches up to the very last minute, but he also knew how to bring his text across with dedication, a bronze voice, and the occasional tear, while shifting his eyes from left to right and from right to left across the teleprompter screens with dignity. Thanks to his media savviness he managed to create a super tight image for himself in image and sound, which strangely enough also gave the impression of being authentic. Thereby showing himself to be a true artist.

Now, if an artist does manage to go beyond the art system, this artist begins to function in the same way that politicians, sports heroes, terrorists, movie stars, and

other minor or major celebrities already function: through the media. In other words, the artist becomes the artwork.

Boris Groys, www.eflux.com

Creating one's own profile in the media is no longer the exclusive privilege of politicians and other stars. Using our laptops and smartphones we can all build our own image and present this image of our own making to the world. Is that fake? No, being able to create our self-image may just as well be seen as a useful defence mechanism, a response to the wave of images coming at us and a way to hold our own in a society that is characterized by increased mobility and leisure time and by an ever-growing number of choices, for example when it comes to gender and other forms of identity.

Design has transformed society itself into an exhibition space in which individuals appear as both artists and self-produced works of art.

Boris Groys, www.eflux.com

Being able to regard mankind as a work of art is not some form of disenchantment. Rather, this makeability underlines the mystic aspect of life, it's intangibility. With self-design we are facing a future in which making a difference becomes the creative challenge. The world will be more colourful, less conventional, more exciting and more imaginative when everyone becomes a designer.

On the one hand, our daily life is boring and our natural identity is very restrictive but, on the other hand, we have a parallel, virtual space to which we can go in order to liberate ourselves, experiment with identities and where we can become someone else in a playful environment.

Sherry Turkle, *The Second Self*

ARE YOU MAKE-ABLE?

BODY

HAVE YOU ALREADY GOT IT? THE MOBILIMB?

'Smartphone with a finger? Augmenting Mobile Devices with a Robotic Limb', youtube.com

OR IS YOUR ARM ITSELF ALREADY PART OF YOUR SMARTPHONE? ☐ YES ☐ NO

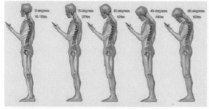 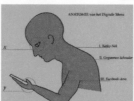 

VERTEBRA ARE CHANGING

By walking upright body parts have changed form and mankind has grown taller and bigger.

YOUR BODY KEEPS EVOLVING.
THE EVOLUTION CONTINUES!

gezondheidenco.nl/why you shouldn't take your phone with you to the bathroom/

10 TIMES MORE MICROBES ON PHONE THAN ON TOILET SEAT

OUR BODIES ARE VAPORIZERS

Lucy McRae, 'How Can Technology Transform the Human Body?, ted.com

A Texan research team has developed a kind of tattoo ink that consists of microparticles that are able to collect and transmit information about your physical health.

Lucy McRae, 'How Can Technology Transform the Human Body?, ted.com

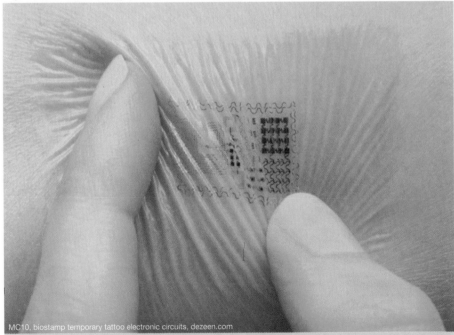

MC10, biostamp temporary tattoo electronic circuits, dezeen.com

WILL YOUR BODY BECOME AN INTERFACE?

ARE YOU READY FOR A *MIXTURE* OF **TO BE AND TO CAN**???

WILL YOU ALLOW TECHNOLOGY INSIDE YOUR BODY?

☐ **YES** ☐ ☐**NO**

MOTIVATE _____

WHAT ADAPTATION WOULD YOU LIKE:

- ☐ Plastic stomachs that can vomit.
- ☐ The waterless, bloodless AWAK (A Wearable Artificial Kidney).
- ☐ Fully artificial hearts that will end organ waiting lists.
- ☐ Artificial lungs that you carry in a backpack.
- ☐ Multi-filament artificial muscles that make humanoid robots more lifelike.
- ☐ Empathy as an extra sense.
- ☐ New artificial skin that can detect heat, just like a rattlesnake.
- ☐ Bionic wings so we can fly
- ☐ A bionic leg that senses when you want to walk, sit, or stand.
- ☐ New cochlear implants that give deaf people an advantage.
- ☐ A bionic eye implant so that blind people can see again.
- ☐ Reprogramming DNA to adapt characteristics.

THE FUSION OF YOU AND THE MACHINE IS NO SCIENCE-FICTION—IT'S REALITY.

'10 technologieën waarmee we op een dag allemaal een beetje cyborg worden',www.richardvanhooijdonk.com

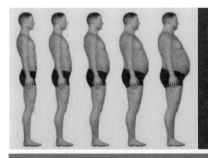

EVEN THOUGH WE KEEP GETTING FATTER, SLIM IS STILL THE IDEAL
Damon Young

Our bodies, with the old genetic transmission, have not kept pace with the new language-produced cultural transmission of technology. So now, when social control breaks down, we must expect to see pathological destruction.

Donna J. Haraway, *Simians, Cyborgs, and Women: The Reinvention of Nature*

CARE OR CONTROL?

IT IS STILL UNCLEAR WHETHER SELF-TRACKING IS GOOD FOR YOU OR FOR THE CONSUMER INDUSTRY

Tamar Sharon, 'Self-Tracking for Health and the Quantified Self: Re-Articulating Autonomy, Solidarity, and Authenticity in an Age of Personalized Healthcare'

[CROSS OUT] ➡ YES/NO **ARE YOU A SELF-TRACKER?**

Look carefully at this picture and think which technology you are using or would like to have. Draw your scheme on the opposite page.

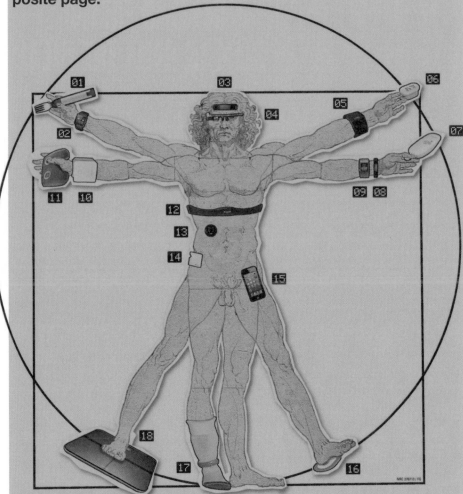

1. Hapifork is a fork that counts bytes in order to set a healthy pace of eating. It also monitors how much you eat each day.
2. Smartwatch. Wireless extension of smartphone for quick reading of incoming messages. Already on the market: Pebble, Sony SmartWatch, I'm Watch, Apple, Microsoft and Samsung are also developing smart watches.
3. SpreeSports headband. Measures body temperature, pulse, and movement to monitor athletic performance.
4. Google Glass projector glasses as hands-free remote control for smartphone.
5. Lark personal sleep coach with sensor in wristband, monitors sleeping pattern.
6. Pulse Oximeter, measures pulse and oxygen content with a sensor around your finger.
7. Glucometer, measures blood sugar level and transmits the result to the iPhone app.
8. Nike Fuel, motion monitor for everyday activities in the shape of bracelet with LEDs. Linked to Nike+ web service.
9. TomTom Sportwatch, monitors motion and location.
10. Bluetooth blood pressure metre in wristband.
11. ECG monitor, works via Bluetooth.
12. Pulse monitor, via Bluetooth.
13. Bio module Zephyr, monitors pulse, breathing, posture, position, and activities.
14. Philips DirectLife activity monitor, carried in a pocket or on a chain.
15. Smartphone: most gadgets transmit the data wireless to apps for android or iPhone.
16. Bluetooth step counter Nike, works with smartphone or sports watch.
17. Smart sock: ankle bracelet with motion monitor that attaches to a sock.
18. Smart body analyser. Smart scales, measures weight, fat content, pulse and the CO_2 content in the environment.

Marc Hijnk, 'Maak je lichaam slim', *NRC Handelsblad*

Draw the technology in your body.

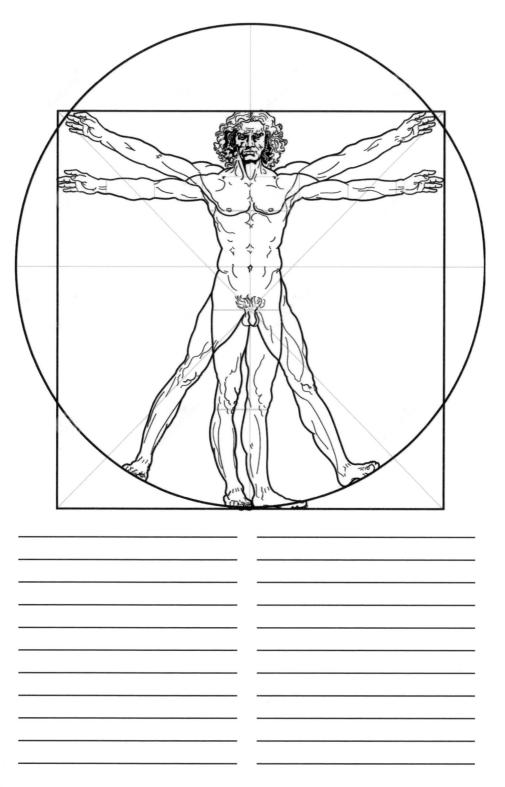

ARE YOU HUMAN OR A ROBOT?

AUTOMATISATION

IS YOUR LIFE A PROGRAMME?

- EVERY DAY YOU GO TO THE SUPERMARKET
- YOU ARE CONSTANTLY CHECKING YOUR PHONE
- YOU ALWAYS BUY THE SAME PRODUCTS
- THE SAME THOUGHTS KEEP COMING BACK
- YOU WORK IS REPETITIVE
- EACH NEW DAY IS LIKE THE LAST ONE

DO YOU TALK TO MACHINES?

SIRI! ALEXA!
where are you?

Geert Lovink

ARE YOU A ROBOT?

● I think I am human

Did you know that your habits and lifestyle are the basis for the robot that you are?

Sometimes we don't realize that in the makeable society we as humans are also already robotized to a high degree. This process has been going on for quite some time and is the result of standardization, mass production, automatization, bureaucracy, and globalization. We have domesticated ourselves; our teeth have shrunk because we cook our food, our muscles are weaker because we use tools, and our fur has lost its hair because we wear clothes and heat our dwellings. Since some thirty years, computers are part of the social and economic structure and now there are algorithms that make sure that your pattern-driven life is continuous. When we buy something online or watch something on Netflix, we think it's our own choice. Well, it turns out that algorithms influence one-third of our decisions. Algorithms have their own biases. They can even go rogue.

Kartik Hosanagar in 'Who Made That Decision: You or an Algorithm?, knowledge.wharton.upenn.edu

PLEASE TICK:

■ **YOUR LIFE IS RUNNING COMPLETELY ON SCHEDULE.**
■ **YOU CAN FEEL YOUR TOES.**
■ **YOU ARE BECOMING NUMB TO WHAT'S INSIDE AND OUTSIDE OF YOURSELF.**
■ **YOU THINK FOR YOURSELF.**
■ **TECHNOLOGY EMBEDS ITSELF IN YOU.**

Image: unknown

Select all images below that match this one

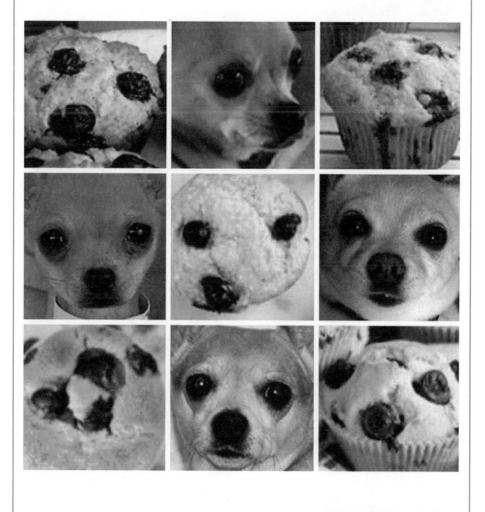

Verify

The machine imitates you and it wants to be able to make and do like you.

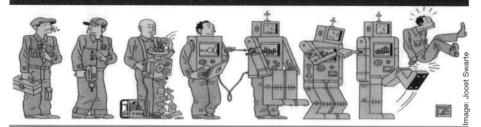

Image: Joost Swarte

WHEN A ROBOT CLEANS YOUR HOUSE IT SHOULD DO SO BETTER THAN YOU.
Koert van Mensvoort

WILL YOU STILL HAVE A JOB?

'In the years to come, technology will lead us to an almost work-free society', wrote Jeremy Rifkin in his classic *The End of Work* (1995). According to Timothy Ferris, for starters we will have a 4-hour workweek. This revolutionary idea points the way to a new life of few working hours, much spare time, and money in abundance, whether you are an overworked wage slave or a businessman who is stuck in the success of his company.

Some evolutionary biologists say that we had better get used to the idea that our human intelligence is not any more special than that of robots. With each scientific breakthrough, man becomes less unique. The invention of the telescope proved we were not the centre of the universe and the advent of evolutionary biology showed we were no creatures of God, and now there are robots to take our place. We are inundated with news articles about robots that are our equals or betters in all kinds of fields. There are now robots that write books, replace dance partners, read the news, and become official citizens. Still, aren't these human qualities ascribed to robots a gross exaggeration?

Siri Beerends, 'Robot ≠ Mens', setup.nl

ROBOTS DON'T FALL ILL, THEY DON'T NEED HOLIDAYS, THEY DON'T TAKE MATERNITY LEAVE AND THEY NEVER COMPLAIN.
Rutger Bregman, 'De race tegen de machine', decorrespondent.nl

YOU ARE A ROBOT MADE BY ROBOTS MADE BY ROBOTS

Daniel Dennett

HOW TO BEHAVE AS A ROBOT:

01 Use monotone speech and short phrases.
02 Maintain a blank expression and blink as little as possible.
03 React only to questions and commands.
04 Avoid showing emotions and using first person speech.
05 Avoid being seen eating, drinking and going to the bathroom.
06 Decide what you're programmed to do and your triggers.
07 Walk slowly.
08 Hold positions for long periods of time.
09 Repeat basic movements.
10 Move body parts independently and maintain good posture.
11 Isolate body parts to dance like a robot.
12 Avoid most smooth movements and gestures
13 Wear the same thing every day.
14 Choose neutral coloured clothing.
15 Avoid accessories and other human behaviours.
16 Apply metallic makeup and stiffen your hair.
17 Keep your face frozen.

'How to act like a robot', wattpad.com

DOMINATE THE MACHINES!

Elbow
Wrist
Shoulder
Tool
Waist

YOU ARE A SNACK FOR THE HUNGRY DATA INDUSTRY THAT WANTS TO BE FED.

Miriam Rasch, *Frictie: Ethiek in tijden van dataïsme*

PLACE A MARK AT EACH OBJECT.

100%
HUMAN(LIKE)
OR NATURAL

100%
SYSTEM
OR ROBOT

DIGITAL ASSISTANT

STOCK MARKET

SMARTWATCH

GLOBALIZATION

INTERNET

ELECTRIC CAR

PENSION

ZOOM

UBER

SOLAR ENERGY

CROSSTRAINER

E-READER

WHATS-APP

MORTGAGE INTEREST RELIEF

HYPER-ALLERGENIC PET

LAWNMOWER ROBOT

VIBRATOR

DO YOU HAVE ANYTHING TO HIDE?

PRIVACY

LOG OFF

HOW TO STAY CONNECTED AFTER DISCONNECTING

PRIVACY IS AN UNPOPULAR PROBLEM OF OUR AGE.

Privacy violation is like a fungus. When left untreated it will overgrow and spoil everything. It demands severe suppression. By society itself, but most certainly also by the Privacy Watchdog. Currently, it looks as if privacy violations are allowed. They are not, and they are punishable by law!

privacyfirst.nl

Image: Waag Society

In China you are tested for COVID-19 and you are issued with a health code for entering shops.

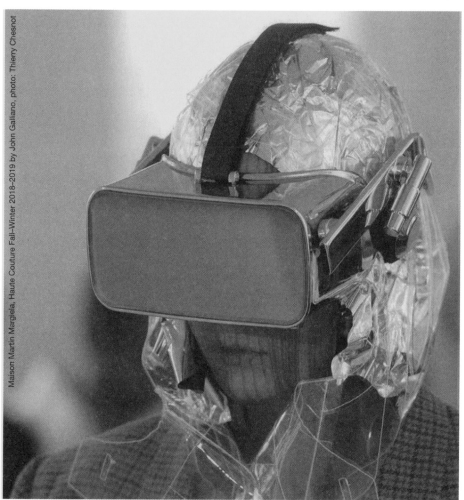

Maison Martin Margiela, Haute Couture Fall-Winter 2018-2019 by John Galliano, photo: Thierry Chesnot

WHAT IS YOUR TAKE ON PRIVACY?

Society is changing. The smartphone is like a mirror you hold up to yourself and nowadays it is *the* tool for shaping your life. We submit all our personal data to social media platforms for free, for fear of missing a Facebook invitation for a party. We click away lengthy privacy updates because we want to get on with our Netflixing. Household privacy doubts we know only too well. That uncertain realization that you haven't got your data in order, have lost your logon codes, and so on. As a societal issue of our times privacy remains abstract, just like the environmental pollution data use causes. But recycling has never become really sexy, even though we all know that is necessary. Privacy is a pleasant social glue, though, allowing us to make a collective fist against lazy government agencies, multinationals, and sometimes even the Russians. It is the domain in which we should put our trust in our government, the designated privacy watchdog of our turbulent times. Unfortunately, not all governments are reliable. ***Start your own investigation!***

Ward Janssen

> Will you be living in a world where myriad data-bases are constantly being filled with information about every step you take, every purchase you make, and every thought you have?
>
> Marleen Stikker

YOU ARE BEING MONITORED.

PRIVACY IS A FUNDAMENTAL RIGHT. A CONDITION TO BE FREE IN WHO YOU ARE AND WHAT YOU DO. PRIVACY IS ABOUT BEING IN CONTROL OF YOUR DATA. IT'S ABOUT NOT BEING CONSTANTLY FOLLOWED, ABOUT YOUR MEDICAL DATA BEING SAFE, ABOUT BEING ABLE TO DO SOMETHING ABOUT AND AUTOMATICALLY TAKE A DECISION ABOUT YOU. IT IS ABOUT OWNING YOUR OWN PERSONAL DATA.

'Waarom is privacy belangrijk?', autoriteitpersoonsgegevens.nl

ARE YOU AWARE OF YOUR SITUATION? *Tick or describe!*

○ You are the biggest privacy denier there is, a fanatical Instagram. Being a full-blooded exhibitionist, your smartphone is your tool of social assertiveness. Selfies, Snapchat filters, Twitter rows, Instagram live feeds and YouTube celebrities. You are addicted to the online success bubble of digital consuming and endless sharing.

○ Your data are not public. You are safe. Privacy is high on your agenda, but at some cost to your consumer happiness. You're using DuckDuckGo instead of Google. You deleted your Facebook account and you check every tool you do use for safety. Giving up privacy may be convenient, but you don't mind missing the odd party.

○ You are extremely privacy-conscious. You do not use a smartphone. You have no apps. You have Internet access on your computer so you can transfer money online, but in shops you pay cash.

Other, namely: _____
_____
_____

WHAT DOES EDWARD SNOWDEN SAY?

'You're sitting here now. Your phone is probably in your pocket, and it's on. So now you can be traced. Your SIM card has a unique number so you can always be reached, almost anywhere in the world. All telephones are continually transmitting a signal: "I'm here." And the telephone pole says: "Yes, I hear you." You were always connected to the nearest antenna and it will reveal your location (approximately)', says Snowden. 'The world is changing, faster than ever. Everything is connected: telephones, workplaces, friends, countries, and in the last instance the entire world.' Snowden talks about how much information about us is already stored and how much is still being stored by companies and governments. 'While authoritarianism is spreading and emergency laws are in place, we are giving up our rights and with them the possibility to prevent that we slip further into a less free world.' 'There is no such thing as a temporary suspension of civil rights. The "temporary measure" always turns out to be permanent. In panic situations liberties disappears quickly if you don't act.'

Edward Snowden in 'Edward Snowden meent dat coronamaatregelen onze vrijheid in gevaar brengen', cursor.tue.nl; 'Snowden: "Overheden gebruiken coronavirus om meer macht te grijpen"', detheorist.nl

IS YOUR FREEDOM AT RISK SINCE COVID-19?

- ☐ The government determines your freedom of movement.
- ☐ A ban on gatherings.
- ☐ Strict controls are on the rise.
- ☐ Enforced quarantine (imprisonment).
- ☐ A ban on cash.
- ☐ Compulsory medical treatment; your body becomes state property.
- ☐ Classification of activities and destinations.

Privacy (a fundamental right) must be built-in in the design of technology. *Privacy by design* must be mandatory when such applications are used.

Marleen Stikker in 'Privacywaakhond', nos.nl

HOW DO YOU DESIGN YOUR PRIVATE SPACE?

IS HOPING FOR WISE POLITICAL DECISIONS THE ONLY THING LEFT TO DO? ARE YOU GOING TO WAIT WHILE CONSUMING HOW THINGS GROW WORSE AND GET COMPLETELY OUT OF CONTROL?

BECOME AWARE OF YOUR SITUATION AND FILL OUT THE DIAGRAM ⟶

ARE YOU ENCAPSULATED BY THE SYSTMES THAT MONITOR YOU?

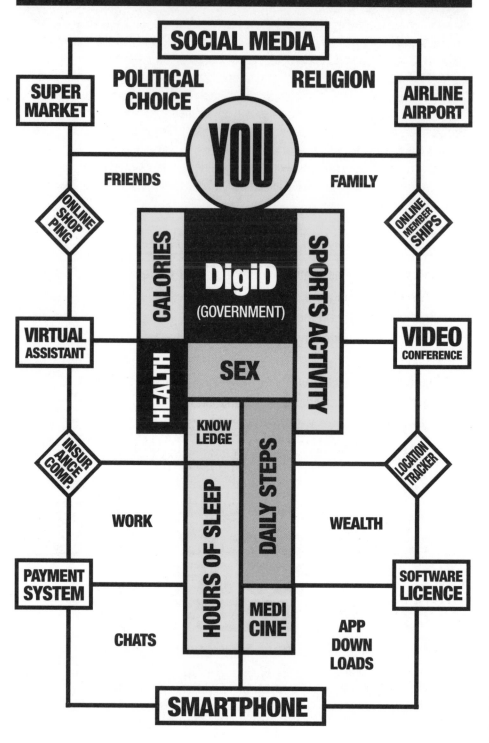

FILL OUT!

AND BECOME AWARE OF YOUR CONTROL SYSTEM.
name companies and organizations, brands and products

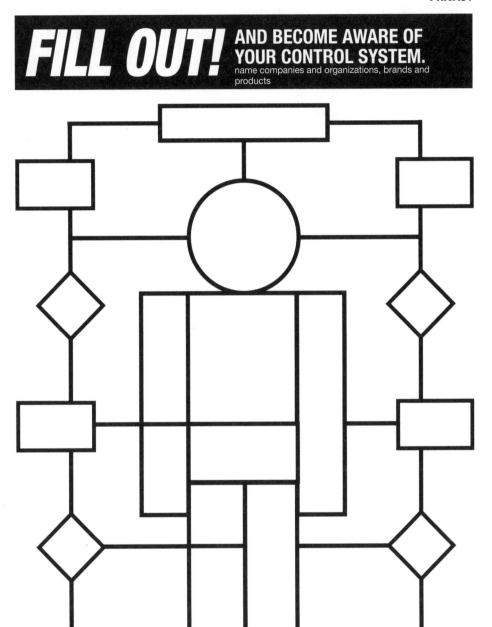

ARE YOU YOUR OWN DOCTOR?

HEALTH

Your human cells are only 10% of the cells in your body. The other 90% are microbes.

Larry Smarr in 'Q&A: The Self-experimenter Who Intends to Change Medicine', zdnet.com

Is obesity contagious?

☐ **YES** ☐ **NO**

MOTIVATE _____

How much candy, pizza and sweets do you buy in the supermarket with your bonus card?

Every day?  Yes

A CULTURE FIXATED ON FEMALE THINNESS IS NOT AN OBSESSION ABOUT FEMALE BEAUTY, BUT AN OBSESSION ABOUT FEMALE OBEDIENCE.

Naomi Wolf, *The Beauty Myth*

ARE YOU WATCHING YOUR MICROBES?

ORTHOREXIA

The only 'unhealthy' extravagance that Anouk still allowed herself allowed herself was one small piece of chocolate a month, and even then only of the variety with 99% cocoa, to avoid too much sugar and fat. The rest of the time she was obsessing about healthy food. Eventually, it turned out she was suffering from orthorexia. She hardly went out any more, as she was spending her days at her laptop doing research into healthy food. At her low point Anouk would spend hours on the Internet looking for what was healthy and what was not and she became completely isolated from the world outside.

Hatixhe Raba, 'Als gezond leven een obsessie wordt', eenvandaag.atavist.com

INFOBESITY

digitaldetoxacademy.eu

WHAT DIET ARE YOU FOL- LOWING?

- Bread diet
- Protein diet
- Cookie diet
- Cambridge diet
- Montignac diet
- Detox diet
- Fruit diet
- Soup diet
- Intestine diet
- Dr Frank diet

- Juice fasting
- Crash diet
- Weight Watchers
- Fitluc diet
- Sonja Bakker diet
- Atkins diet
- Dreamline diet
- Ten-day diet
- Banana diet
- One-day diet

- Vegetarian diet
- Blood group diet
- Keto diet
- Fat-free diet
- Anti-diet
- Egg diet
- Libelle diet
- Alpha diet
- Garcina Cambogia diet

◖MEDIA DIET

CITIZENS ARE ENTITLED TO DARKNESS; TO BE FAT AND UNHEALTHY IS A FREE CHOICE.

Paul Frissen

SO, DON'T LET THEM DRIVE YOU CRAZY! IF YOU'RE HAPPY AND YOU ARE TOO FAT THEN JUST STAY FAT AND HAPPY.

BUT IF YOU ARE TOO FAT AND YOU DON'T LIKE IT, THEN DON'T FORGET THIS:

DIETS DON'T WORK!

IT'S ALL ABOUT MENTALITY!

FROM BURGER KING

USA TODAY

Becoming used to a simple and sober eating pattern contributes to our health. It makes us resilient against the hardships that life inevitably confronts us with and provides us with a solid foundation when after times of scarcity we experience abundance.

– Epicurus

A Whopper with no preservatives, colors or flavors from artificial sources, eu.usatoday.com

HEALTH HOLIDAYS

title
juice fasting
organization

4590 STEPS

DO YOU KNOW YOUR ONLINE HEALTH FILE?
IT REALLY EXISTS!

The Internet of Things technology makes it easier for people to control their own lifestyle without having to consult their doctor about everything. It becomes easier for both patients and doctors to monitor a patient's progress and follow-up treatment. A growing number of patients are going about wearing so-called 'wearables', portable items that provide regular updates about their health. For example, a diabetes patient may carry a device that constantly communicates with his or her smartphone. This allows the patient to always — and in great detail — check their blood sugar level and anticipate by, for example, injecting insulin. In some cases, these patient data are even transmitted to a cloud service to which their doctor also has access. This means that in certain situations the doctor will immediately receive an online alert when a patient's blood pressure suddenly rises in an alarming way.

Ina Danova, 'IoT: een nieuw tijdperk voor gezondheidszorg', pegus.digital/nl; 'Big data binnen de gezondheidszorg: hoe zit dat precies', tottadatalab.nl

DO YOU TEST YOURSELF?

DO YOU BECOME HEALTHIER IF YOU KNOW MORE ABOUT YOURSELF?

YES   NO

LIVE IN JOY AND HEALTH, EVEN IF THE WHOLE WORLD IS ILL.

BUDDHA

Do you know your inner self?

Fritz Kahn, *Der Mensch als Industriepalast*, 1926, Stuttgart: Fricke & Co.

DESIGN YOUR OWN HEALTHY BURGER

Fill the burger with ingredients, kcal, grams

1.

2.

3.

4.

5.

6.

7.

8.

9.

10.

11.

12.

Use only healthy ingredients! For example, use lettuce instead of bread.

WHAT ARE YOU?

IDENTITY

TICK WHAT APPLIES TO YOU.

- [ ] **I THINK**
- [ ] **I FEEL**
- [ ] **I WORK**
- [ ] **I'M CALLED**
- [ ] **I BELONG**
- [ ] **I SUFFER**
- [ ] **I HAVE A PAST**
- [ ] **I AM NICE**
- [ ] **I AM RECOGNIZED**
- [ ] **I CONSUME**
- [ ] **I HAVE A BODY**
- [ ] **I AM MYSELF**

Content page from Stine Jensen and Rob Wijnberg, *Dus ik ben: Een zoektocht naar identiteit*

NO FACE.

Your face is not your private property. Each time you look into a camera or talk to the digital assistant you give away a little piece of your self. When faces and voices are being used or abused on a massive scale, we have an identity crisis on our hands. It will be almost impossible to prove any more who you are, when your face and your voice are no longer yours.

Sander Duivestein, Thijs Pepping en Menno van Doorn, 'Laat de grip op uw identiteit niet aan techbedrijf over', *de Volkskrant*

Face masks which were created by reverse engineering facial recognition and detection algorithms.

Want to know what your face looks like?
Then work with a code programmer!

Sterling Crispin, data masks, sterlingcrispin.com

YOUR IDENTITY IS DIGITAL.

Your identity will increasingly become your life story, complete with political leaning, religion, the balance in your bank account, and who your friends are. Online it will just be your 'social presence', later, through algorithms, it will be your trump when applying for a mortgage, your Social Security number, and passport information. Your footprint has been in the making for at least twenty years. To understand the challenges and opportunities digital innovation brings to identity, we have to look at the foundational concept of identity. Each person is multi-faceted — you're a composite of your biological, behavioural, personality, and character traits. Have you ever opened a savings account? Taken out a loan? Used a credit card?

Adapted source: Priya Punatar, 'What Is Identity and Why Does It Matter?', medium.com

CHOOSE YOUR COLOUR

| 255 220 177 | 229 194 152 | 228 185 142 | 226 185 143 | 227 161 115 | 217 145 100 | 204 132 67 | 199 122 88 | 165 57 0 | 134 4 0 |
| #FFDCB1 | #E5C298 | #E4B98E | #E2B98F | #E3A173 | #D99164 | #CC8443 | #C77A58 | #A53900 | #880400 |

ARE YOU QUEER OR DRAG?

NON-BINARY & GENDERFLUID

PANSEXUAL?

0   1   2   3   4   5   6   7   8
9

LGBTQ+ ⊗ ✓

YES ◯ ◯ NO

YOU DON'T IDENTIFY AS ANYTHING, YOU ARE A PERSON

THEY SHE ZE HE XE

OUR 'SELF', OUR OWN IDENTITY IS NOW A COMMODITY OR COMPANY THAT WE ENTER THE MARKET WITH.

Thijs Lijster, 'Levenskunst als handelswaar', *Mister Motley*

SELFMADE?

Paul B Preciado   Gigi Gorgeous   Cara Delevingne

It's limiting, that LGBTQ thing. It served a function as an umbrella for marginalized people to whom rights were being denied, but it loses its efficacy because of the nuanced nature of humanity. As we become more educated and expand the facts of our nature, we keep adding letters. It was a great shield, but now we're stuck behind it. It's so important to resist labels. I don't care how many letters you add. At some point, it's going to spell 'WE ARE HUMAN'.

Amber Heard in 'Why Amber Heard Said She Was "So Wrong, Just So Wrong"', *Allure Magazine*

'Identify as We' campaign by Sephora. Image: Craig and Carl/Sephora

NORMCORE:

The cultural trendsetters are all trading in their designer clothes for practical non-aesthetic, as an act of rebellion against the display of success, exclusivity and cultural elitism.

Steve Jobs

Angela Merkel

Mark Zuckerberg

Mass taste as statement

Normcore, a term coined by the New York artists collective K-Hole, described an ultra-hip trend of conscious inconspicuousness as a social protest against a success-driven world that felt like a commercial echo of reality; a new reality of being normal, hardcore normal.

HOW NORMCORE ARE YOU?

NORMCORE 9 8 7 6 5 4 3 2 1 0 PROMCORE

WHO DESIGNS YOUR IDENTITY?

YOU did not create the materials out of which it is formed. They are odds and ends of thoughts, impressions, feelings, gathered unconsciously from a thousand books, a thousand conversations, and from streams of thought and feeling which have flowed down into your heart and brain out of the hearts and brains of centuries of ancestors. PERSONALLY you did not create even the smallest microscopic fragment of the materials out of which your opinion is made; and personally you cannot claim even the slender merit of PUTTING THE BORROWED MATERIALS TOGETHER. That was done AUTOMATICALLY — by your mental machinery, in strict accordance with the law of that machinery's construction. And you not only did not make that machinery yourself, but you have NOT EVEN ANY COMMAND OVER IT.

Mark Twain, *What is Man*

YOU ARE A MEME!

You think, because you repeat the thoughts of other people, because you borrow from history and plagiarize the ideas of your teachers. You think, because you are influenced and because you focus on the thoughts that were poured into your head through the exchange with other people. You think, because you articulate the thoughts of others in a slightly different form and then you call it your own opinion.

Joost Meerloo, *Het web van menselijke en sociale relaties*

DO YOU NOT WANT TO BELONG ANYWHERE?

YES ○
NO ○

OR YOU DON'T BELONG ANYWHERE?

YES ○
NO ○

THEARTOFINBETWEEN

FOR WHOM DO YOU MAKE YOURSELF BEAUTIFUL?

BEAUTY

IN A CULTURE WHERE MANIPULATED IMAGES ARE THE NORM YOUR SELF IMAGE IS UNDER ENORMOUS PRESSURE.

Radboud Gender & Diversity Studies, ru.nl

'You are not born as a woman. You are made into one.'

THE WOMAN IS A DESIGN OF THE MAN

Simone de Beauvoir, *The Second Sex*

IS FEMINISM STILL ALIVE?

WHEN A WOMAN WEARS LIPSTICK SHE IS REALLY A FRAUD.

Koert van Mensvoort

FOR WHOM DO YOU MAKE YOURSELF BEAUTIFUL?

FOR YOURSELF

FOR SOMEONE ELSE

In antiquity, the general opinion was that beauty could only exist in relation to what was morally right. *Have you let go of that connection?*

ARE YOU A BEAUTY PRODUCT?

There was a time when we were part of nature, but since modern society has characterised as individuals, we turn out to be the creative creator of ourselves. The current social pressure to design yourself is being under-estimated. We have the complex task of working on ourselves to obtain the desired result. This is both a responsible and an artistic mission. We want to do it in our own characteristic way and so we can only rely on our own sense of aesthetics and our imagination and how we let ourselves be influenced by media.

Not all of us are ready to tolerate humanoid creatures with plastic faces, power-driven limbs, and microchip implants in our environment. Cosmetic surgery is about more than just appearances, in many cases. By being more beautiful, we gain self-confidence and feel better. Nowadays we consider natural beauty as the ideal, as is evident from the cult success of the make-up and skin care brand Glossier. Women who look pore-less and radiant and are ruthlessly beautiful in front of an iPhone camera, even without make up. But this so-called natural beauty is totally fabricated, the interventions and products are completely invisible. The beauty ideal is a source of strength and control to exercise power, though at the cost of a great number of people, so far: women often only make more money than men from porn, modelling, and Instagram influencing.

Ward Janssen

Kim and Kourtney Kardashian in Blue Lagoon Iceland, 2016

BUT

if you want to be really beautiful:

- labia correction
- breast implants
- stomach reduction
- penis extension
- facelift
- abdominal wall correction
- chest muscle enhancement
- testosterone suppletion
- hormone therapy
- hair transplant

ARE YOU A PHARMABORG OR A CYBORG?

LYCRA, SPANDEX AND POLYAMID LIFT YOUR BUTTOCKS AND EXTREMELY ACCENTUATE YOUR BREASTS!

IT HAS LONG BEEN KNOWN THAT CLOTHING AFFECTS HOW OTHER PEOPLE PERCEIVE YOU, AS WELL AS HOW YOU THINK ABOUT YOURSELF.

Adam Galinsky

ONCE UPON A TIME, SOCIETY CONSIDERED THAT IT KNEW WHAT WAS BEAUTIFUL: Young, white, straight, cis, thin, symmetrical, Eurocentric and stereo-typically feminine — plus long, golden hair, if at all possible, although exceptions might be made for the occasional raven-haired temptress. CASES OF RACISM, SEXISM, indeed, ANYTHING-AT-ALL-ISM are rightly considered unacceptable, and 'CHAL-LENGING ACCEPTED BEAUTY STANDARDS' is the phrase du jour. One is no longer allowed to discriminate over age, gender, ethnicity, reli-gion, physical and mental ability, sexual orienta-tion, education or national origin—anything, in fact, that might inspire prejudice in the tunnel-visioned—meaning our definitions of beauty are suddenly a lot more woke.

Hannah Betts, 'How Diversity Became the New Beauty Ideal', stylist.co.uk

HOW DIVERSITY BECAME THE NEW BEAUTY IDEAL

HUMANE BEAUTY

Long before 40 shades became the gold standard and historically white-centric brands touted inclusivity and diversity, Black women were the only ones meeting the oft-overlooked needs of our community. They were the only ones with shade ranges, cast-free sunscreens, and a catalog to define 'nude'. We must continue to strive for diversity and inclusivity within the beauty industry and support the companies by us and for us who are doing the tireless work to spotlight, enrich, and highlight all that is wonderfully Black and beautiful.

Taylor Davis a.o., '22 Black-Owned Skincare Brands to Support Now and Forever', elle.com

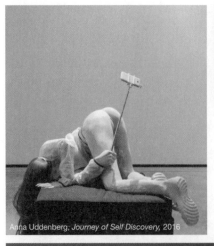

Anna Uddenberg, *Journey of Self Discovery*, 2016

TIPS FOR THE PERFECT SELFIE

The selfie, like all technology, causes us to reflect on our human values. This is a good thing because it challenges us to figure out what they really are.

Sherry Turkle, 'The Documented Life', *The New York Times*

1. Never photograph yourself point blank. It makes your face look really flat. **2. Hold the camera a little higher than your head.** It usually makes a difference of 10 years and 10 kilos. **3. Stand near a window.** Preferably in the famous northern light. **4. Hold your chin very slightly down.** If you have read Tip 2, take your picture at an angle from above. **5. Check your background.** Pick a nicely even, quiet background. **6. Turn off your flash.** Flash from nearby is terribly unflattering. **7. NO DUCK FACE.** You will make a fool of yourself. **8. Breathe in, and especially also breathe out.** This will relax your face and the rest of your body. **9. Enjoy the process.** In digital photography you can do it again many times. **10. Use a nice filter.** Don't be ashamed. Everyone does it.

Else Kramer, 'Tien tips voor de perfecte selfie', elskramer.nl

DESCRIBE YOUR BEAUTY

YOUR MOUTH

YOUR IMAGINATION

YOUR SEX

YOUR HANDS

YOUR TASTE

YOUR GLANCE

YOUR CHARACTER

YOUR THOUGHTS

YOUR LEGS

YOUR HAIRDO

DO YOU LOVE YOURSELF?

LOVE

GIVING TAKING SEDUCING
KISSING MARRYING FEELING
FINDING WANTING OWNING
CARESSING CRYING DIVORCING
HATING BALANCING GIVING
TAKING SEDUCING KISSING
MARRYING FEELING FINDING
WANTING OWNING CARESSING
CRYING DIVORCING HATING

IS LOVE AN ARRANGEMENT?
☐ YES ☐ NO

MOTIVATE _____

There is only one form of love that should last an eternity *and that is self-love.*

ACCORDING TO MOST SELF-HELP BOOKS YOU MUST FIRST LOVE YOURSELF BEFORE YOU CAN LOVE SOMEONE ELSE.
Svend Brinkmann

BUT IS THAT TRUE? WHOEVER SAID IT WAS SO?

ARE YOU LOOKING FOR LOVE ONLINE?

*THERE ARE PLENTY OF INTERESTING AND NICE PEOPLE WHO'D LIKE TO PAY FOR A FIRST DATE WITH YOU! **PAY PER DATE!***

THIS IS ALL QUITE DEPRESSING, BUT AT THIS POINT I'D JUST LIKE TO ENLIGHTEN YOU WITH THE FOLLOWING QUOTE I CAME ACROSS ON INSTAGRAM:

Every relationship will get 'boring' after you've been together for years. Love isn't a feeling, it's a commitment; to love every day, physically and emotionally. It's difficult, it's not always laughs, smiles and fun. People tend to quit when it stops being fun, and they go look for someone else. 'Oh, the spark is gone.' No, that's not how it works. You want somebody to never give up on you, and love you unconditionally? Do the same. Be the change. This isn't Hollywood, this isn't the movies. That shit isn't real. Love somebody when you don't want to. When they are being a fucking asshole. When they're being hard to love. That's the realist shit there is.

Rhiannon Hutchings, 'Love in the Age of Consumerism', laviederhi.com

Jon Rafman

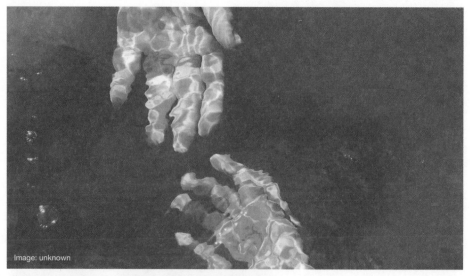

Image: unknown

THE NOVEL

And time and again I will hold your hand and sometimes the palm of yours lies flat and straight against mine as if you want to hold as large a surface as possible of yourself against me … And time and again I will enter you and you will ask me to do so and when you are open to me and will hold me something of a promise of the beauty has been fulfilled after all, the beauty in which we really immerse ourselves with the same expectations and shared thoughts and also our sweat and the fear and the incomprehensible complexity of what else there is of your lips and of my tongue, always searching the same area for something beautiful … And it is warm and moist and dry and hard and soft and cool and when your lips are rough they tear open my soul, making me bleed softly with emotion for you and all the things that you are, all that quiet splendour you offer me because you don't really know what to do with it yourself and all that is almost too much for me and I would like to cry in the nape of your neck, very quietly, you will only feel my tears running down your chest because you are so heartrendingly beautiful and so moving and because I love your thoughts so much and all the unfathomable things going on inside you, moving to the phases of the moon, the pulsing and pounding and the ripeness of autumns and days late in summer like grapes before they are pressed so full and intoxicating is your smell or your presence are your small gestures and your glance your smile your long legs and all that they enclose and protect which gives lives and consolation and rapture like the world in your eyes and behind the unruly fringe of your freshly washed hair.

Geerten Meijsing, *Confessioni di un malandrino* (abbreviated)

LOVE OF THINGS OR PEOPLE.

Iris Murbach (Irish philosopher) gives the example of learning the Russian language, which also requires a kind of love. Learning Russian is a difficult task with a faraway goal that may very well never be reached in full. While she does her best to learn Russian, something that exists independently of her (the Russian language) is slowly being revealed. Attention is rewarded with knowledge of reality. The love of Russian takes her away from herself, toward something that is alien to her.

However, the love of a language is of course different from the love of a person. The Russian language is no individual and the love between people is the love between individuals. You love someone else as a whole (the word 'individual' comes from the Latin word for 'indivisible'). You don't love a random combination of characteristics that can be separated, such as length, weight, personality traits, and so on. 'It may very well be that someone other than the person you love is stronger, slimmer, cleverer, taller, or whatever, but love is not based on such qualities or the sum total of them.'

Taking this as our premise there is something wrong with how we now look for a lover, as it presents the 'self' as a set of more or less measurable qualities. 'We look for a partner who exactly meets our requirements, but this means that the other can simply be reduced to the sum of their qualities and these can always be improved, or other people can be found who possess these qualities to a higher degree.' According to Murbach we love especially that which cannot be simply replaced by something else. For instance, an old worn-out chair in our home that we love so much that we don't want to dispose of it even though there are so much better chairs available. We love an individual person or thing: not the sum of its or their qualities.

Tom Hofland, 'De liefde is geen gevoel (volgens deze filosoof)', bedrock.nl

Alexis Christodoulou, *Imagined Architectural Spaces*, 2017-2020

TRUE LOVE

Robert Indiana, *Love*, 1967

I allow nothing to harm the union of soulmates. True Love doesn't change, not even if we change sides and it does not disappear through separation or grief.

This makes her a steady beacon in the path of any storm, without ever trembling, and for each wavering ship the star that can be ascribed height but not value.

Love is no temporary folly: even as Time will soon fell usefulness,
Love endures this unequal battle;
it will count until the end of days

If any fault in this is ever proven
one has never loved, nor has one read me.

For centuries sonnets have been teaching as how lyrical and nourishing love can be. Shakespeare is our oldest and most prominent poet to put into words full of detail and special beauty that special moment full of detail and poetic beauty in which you recognize your love for your loved one as the greatest moment in life.
Shakespeare's Sonnets. fmlekens.home.xs4all.nl

Banksy, *Love Is In The Air (Flower Thrower)*, 2005

HOW BELOVED ARE YOU?

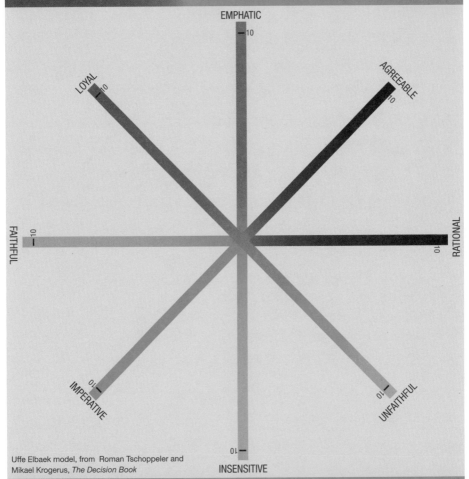

Uffe Elbaek model, from Roman Tschoppeler and
Mikael Krogerus, *The Decision Book*

PLACE A POINT ON EACH LINE AND CONNECT THEM.
Have your partner or a friend also fill out the test.

HOW EXTENDED IS YOUR FAMILY

FAMILY

you have family.

WHO DO YOU RESEMBLE?

WHEN YOU SMILE

MOVE THINK

COMMUNICATE

EAT CRY LIVE

PROCREATE

HAVE YOU STARTED A FAMILY YET?

There isn't a more persistent stereotype than family in the traditional, or rather, archaic sense. It comes with the unwritten social rule that your life is not a success until you have started one yourself. The fact that family as such has long since ceased to be the golden rule is ignored with a shrug. We can dismiss it as a cliché: the family in the coffee brand commercial, the longing for it is still very much alive, something the advertisement branch has grasped only too well. On the other hand, the one-person household is increasingly the norm. Nowhere is the Tinder app used as much as in one-person households. Purely for sex? Out of the wish to have a partner, or out of social guilt feelings?

Ward Janssen

78

WE CHAT

DAD — 6m ago
Forecasters predict "insane" crop of tomatoes this year, leading people to wonder if you would like some.

MOM — 20m ago
😀😂🤚💀💀💀🐷

MOM — 22m ago
Correction: The previous message should have read "hello," not a string of those little picture guys.

SISTER — 14s ago
The President made another controversial statement at the White House. Did you see this shit?

MOM — 1m ago
Two New Yorkers were hurt in a traffic accident, raising questions: Was this near you? Are you O.K.?

MOM — 3m ago
The 2020 flu season is worse than ever. Have you gotten your shot? They're free at the CVS or the Walgreens; call after you've gone. Remember how sick your cousin got?

GRANDPARENTS — 12m ago
Florida residents awaken this morning to the reality that a visit is out of the question, but a phone call would be nice.

James Folta, 'Push Notifications from Your Family', newyorker.com

Chloe usually kept herself in the background in the group app, not posting much. When family members shared things she didn't agree with, she would always try to avoid conflict — until one day she noticed something she just couldn't ignore.

'I usually keep quiet', says Chloe. 'But I really had to say something when a remark was made about migrants. That's when I objected.'

It didn't turn out well. 'My brother told me to bugger off and that he was ashamed that I was part of "their" family. My sister agreed with him, and my parents said nothing. And then my brother threw me out of the group.'

Ruby Lott-Lavigna, 'The Highs and Lows of the Family Group App', vice.com

IN HOW MANY FAMILY-APPS ARE YOU?

1. _____ 2. _____ 3. _____ 4. _____

   ☆☆☆☆☆

HOW MANY STARS DO YOU GIVE YOUR FAMILY?

Photo: Anna Ciolina

The nuclear family is a 20th-century construction

WHAT WILL THE FAMILY OF THE FUTURE BE LIKE?

Family is not only the place where you usually end up when you're born, it is also something you have to put up with all your life. In English the traditional family is called the 'nuclear' family. It means a family with a father, a mother and one or more children, but it sounds as if the traditional family is Chernobyl-proof.

For now, it is no obstacle for assertive citizens in shaping their families.

Now that we no longer need surrogate mothers to make children, the options are endless and you can go all the way in imagining your ideal family. How would you like it to be? Shaping your family is your personal design assignment. Children as a design project! A strong pedigree is after all not something you want to leave to chance; a bit of genetic tweaking produces happy dimples in cheeks or beautiful green eyes. Family happiness can be produced and perfected digitally. Reality can only be disappointing. It often is now also, after all.

Ward Janssen

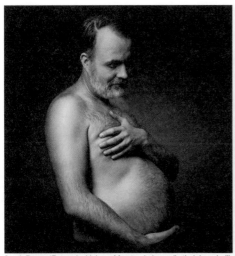
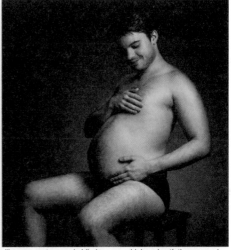

Sarah Barns, 'Brewed with love: Men tenderly cradle their beer bellies like pregnant mums in hilarious new drinks advert', thesun.co.uk

THE ARTIFICIAL WOMB WILL ASK US TO QUESTION CONCEPTS OF GENDER AND PARENTHOOD.

Patricia Piccinini, *The Comforter*, 2010

WE ENTER THE AGE OF ROGUE FAMILIES

Now that the human body is makeable, both before and after birth, the difference between men and women disappears.

Mieke Gerritzen

THERE IS THE POSSIBILITY OF A HUMAN SPECIES WITH A MODULAR BODY

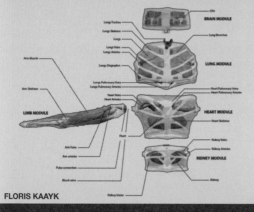

FLORIS KAAYK

Medical technology is working hard at not only producing the customized fusion of the desired prodigy but also its capacities and looks.

IS TECHNOLOGY CREATING A FAMILY DIVIDE?

MAKE UP YOUR OWN FAMILY [TREE]

WHAT QUALITIES WILL YOU PASS ON?

Genes, memes, DNA, behaviour, build, character, knowledge, taste, colour, and more.

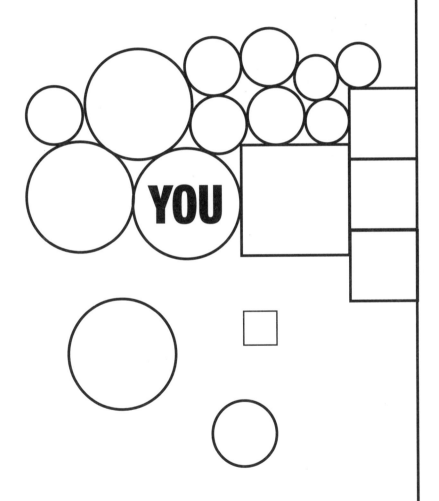

Use: arrows, lines, planes, text, your network, images, and especially your creative power.

DO YOU HAVE DIGITAL SEX?

SEX

sex is everywhere

ON EVERYONE'S MIND

IT MOVES

caresses melts **fills**

French-kisses **desires** blows

pumps cries out

stops eats pussy goes

slides **drips** hesitates

turns pushes sucks

thrusts **caresses** drools pants

comes **bites** licks kisses

SEX IS LANGUAGE

Sex scenes are all about rhythm. He's looking for words that sound the way sex feels. As in the following, more explicit fragment from *Lady Chatterley's Lover*. ... all his blood-vessels seemed to scald with intense yet tender desire, for her, for her softness, for the penetrating beauty of her in his arms, passing into his blood. And softly, with that marvellous swoon-like caress of his hand in pure soft desire, softly he stroked the silky slope of her loins, down, down between her soft warm buttocks, coming nearer and nearer to the very quick of her. And she felt him like a flame of desire, yet tender, and she felt herself melting in the flame.

Julie Phillips, 'Een opwindende scène', *Trouw*

With his fingers as brave little soldiers marching, roaming, stopping now and then, thinking, hesitating... Then marching forward to the soft blood-purple hills, losing themselves in the tiny hairs, caught, going down, slipping inside, sniffing, curious about that place that is like the tiny rabbit hole (down the rabbit hole), diving, sliding up and down, mmm-mmm, with the dark comes fulfilment, go deeper, go greater, go fiercer, don't leave room for anything else, mmmmmmm until the cock, the penis, the prick, the dick, the Schwanz, the rod, the velvet hunter, the ermine, the *kurats* explodes in a glorious mini volcanic eruption of semen and fluid.

Manon Uphoff, *Vallen is als vliegen*

WHAT DO YOU WANT?

It can be wonderful to indulge in sexual arousal.
Why allow yourself a good meal or a good session in the gym, but
not some hot sex with yourself?

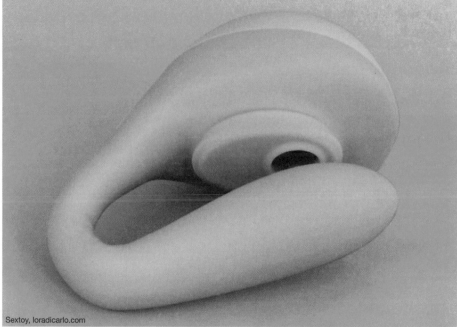

Sextoy, loradicarlo.com

SOLO SEX?

People used to think that masturbation would lead to blindness, infertility or impotency. Let's
be clear: that is not true. You can masturbate to your heart's desire.

SEX ON SUNDAY?

YouPorn user statistics show that their databases are really going into top gear on
Sundays, right after Americans have been to church. Or perhaps it is mostly non-
churchgoers who have slept in.

QUEER SEX?

INSPIRING TO EXPLORE YOUR OWN CONCEPTS OF INTIMACY AND SEXUALITY

IS ROBOT SEX THE FUTURE?

Micro-robotics can simulate the feel of the human mouth, tongue, and fingers to create an intense as possible orgasm.

'Verbannen seksspeeltje "voor intens orgasme" keert terug en verrast iedereen op techbeurs', *Algemeen Dagblad*

JUST IMAGINE:

After a long day at the office, a man flumps onto the couch, ready to masturbate. But instead of his hand, he uses technological tools. He mounts a 'masturbator' over his erection; it's a device that simulates sexual movements, so he doesn't have to do anything himself. On his head he places a gas mask. Today he opts for the odour cartridge 'body scent'. To complete the experience, he dons his virtual reality glasses and picks a porn movie. He is now in a penthouse with an idyllic view of the beach. Looking down, he notices that the couch he's sitting on is now made of white leather. And he's naked. Music pours from the loudspeakers — its smooth jazz — and he hears giggling in the hallway. Four women enter the room, all looking longingly at him. Three of them start to strip, the fourth one pleases him orally. The contracting of his masturbator corresponds exactly with the up-and-down movements of her head. He smells a waft of her perfume. He is the main character in his own porn movie — and all that from the comfort of his own living room.

Dorien van Linge, 'Masturberen doe je in de 21ste eeuw met alle zintuigen', *de Volkskrant*

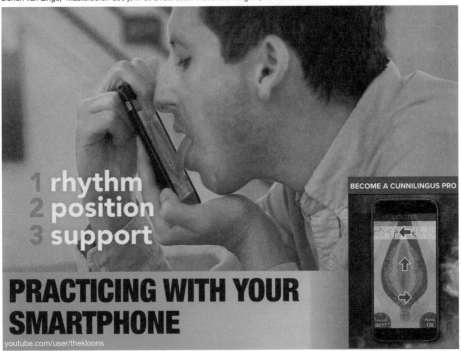

1 **rhythm**
2 **position**
3 **support**

BECOME A CUNNILINGUS PRO

LICKSTER

PRACTICING WITH YOUR SMARTPHONE

youtube.com/user/thekloons

HOW DO YOU DESIGN YOUR SEX LIFE?

Words simply provide more space to develop and use your own images.

H.M. van den Brink

Writing sex, anyway. Are you ready? Then I'll start caressing with my letters, sucking sweetly with my sentences. And then, when you are open and willing to receive, I'll pump my opinions straight into your soft, advice seeking little brains. I will Nouveaufuck you so hard that you will scream with reading pleasure. But in style, Fuckers. Always in style.

Stella Bergsma, *Nouveau Fuck*

WRITE!!!!!!!!!
YOUR OWN SEX SCENE!

ARE YOU STILL LIVING TOGETHER?

COMMUNITY

Is this your Life?

Online you talk to each other, *but not with each other.*

THERE'S A REASON VIDEO APPS MAKE YOU FEEL AWKWARD AND UNFULFILLED.

DO YOU SUFFER FROM SKIN HUNGER?

When we touch, our bodies produce oxytocin, also known as the cuddle or love hormone. It gives a feeling of bonding and connection.

Karine Hoenderdos, 'Huidhonger in tijden van corona', gezondheidsnet.nl

NOWADAYS WE TOUCH EACH OTHER LESS AND LESS, WHICH MEANS THAT WE SATISFY OUR DAILY NEED OF TOUCH LESS AND LESS.

Rosa Bertram, 'Al van huidhonger gehoord?', bedrock.nl

In our age of individualism, we see computers as ways through which we can express our in-dividuality. But the truth is that the computers are really good at spotting the very opposite. The computers can see how similar we are, and they then have the ability to agglomerate us together into groups that have the same behaviours.

Adam Curtis

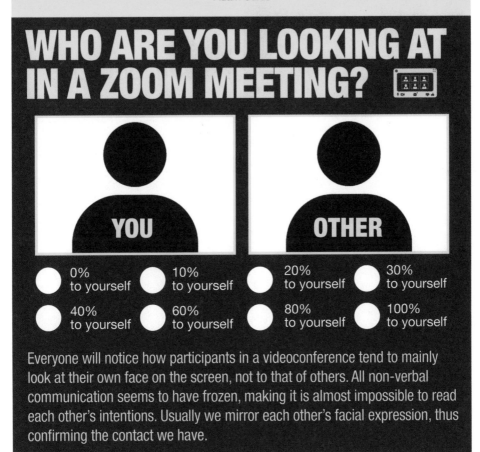

WHO ARE YOU LOOKING AT IN A ZOOM MEETING?

YOU

OTHER

○ 0% to yourself   ○ 10% to yourself   ○ 20% to yourself   ○ 30% to yourself

○ 40% to yourself   ○ 60% to yourself   ○ 80% to yourself   ○ 100% to yourself

Everyone will notice how participants in a videoconference tend to mainly look at their own face on the screen, not to that of others. All non-verbal communication seems to have frozen, making it is almost impossible to read each other's intentions. Usually we mirror each other's facial expression, thus confirming the contact we have.

Stevo Akkerman, 'Zoomen, skypen, meeten, appen, hangouten en andere thuiswerkgruwelen', Trouw;
Kate Murphy, 'Why Zoom Is Terrible', *The New York Times*

WITHOUT REALIZING IT, THE INDIVIDUAL COMPOSES HIS OWN LIFE ACCORDING TO THE LAWS OF BEAUTY, EVEN IN TIMES OF THE GREATEST DISTRESS.

Milan Kundera, *The Unbearable Lightness of Being*

WAS THE LOCKDOWN GOOD FOR YOUR CREATIVITY?

YES, because

_____
_____
_____
_____

NO, because

_____
_____
_____
_____
_____

The COVID-19 virus has totally upset our relation to others. It does make us creative, though, even if we are not always aware of it. Some supermarkets have carried through the 1.5 metre distance so rigorously with tape, stickers, text, and routing that the shop looks like a designer's festival. And facemasks generate a whole new market for the fashion industry. In elevators we stand facing the wall.

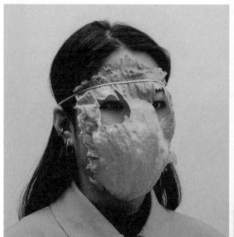

Max Siedentopf, *How-To Survice a Deadly Global Virus*, 2020

SUFFERING FROM REALNESS

JAY-Z (2011)

One of the saddest pictures on the Internet during the COVID-19 crisis.

ARE YOU REALLY GOING DIGITAL NOW, SIMPLY BECAUSE THAT'S ALL THERE IS?

ARE YOU ALSO STARTING AN ONLINE FACEMASK BUSINESS?

Know what to do when you meet a 'human being'

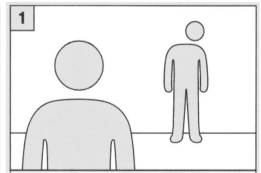

DO THE ONLINE TEST: BENADERING.NL

Martijn Engelbregt, circusengelbregt.nl

Screenshot from Adam Curtis, *HyperNormalisation*, 2016. Courtesy of BBC. Chewing gum: Alexander Husenbeth

HyperNormalisation
BE SOCIAL!
STAY ONLINE!

THE SPECTACLE IS NOT A COLLECTION OF IMAGES; IT IS A SOCIAL RELATION BETWEEN PEOPLE THAT IS MEDIATED BY IMAGES.

Guy Debord, *The Society of the Spectacle*

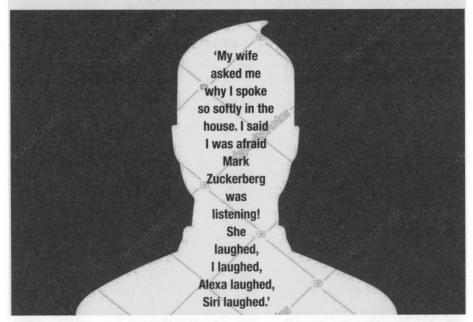

'My wife asked me why I spoke so softly in the house. I said I was afraid Mark Zuckerberg was listening! She laughed, I laughed, Alexa laughed, Siri laughed.'

DO YOU LAUGH?

DOES TECHNOLOGY AFFECT YOUR SOCIAL BEHAVIOUR?

DO YOU APP AT NIGHT?

☐ **YES** ☐ **NO**

DO YOU HAVE FRIENDS YOU DON'T KNOW?

☐ 500+

☐ 1000+

☐ 2000+

DOES THE INTERNET OF THINGS MAKE YOUR WORLD BIGGER?

☐ I HAVE MORE CONTACTS

☐ I THINK IT'S COSY

☐ IT MAKES ME AWARE

☐ I'M VERY VISIBLE

WHERE IS HOME?

HOME

HOME IS WHERE THE WIFI CONNECTS AUTOMATICALLY

Many dystopias already imagine a similar future: we stay at home, work on our computers, communicate through videoconferences, exercise on a machine in the corner of our home office, occasionally masturbate in front of a screen displaying hardcore sex, and get food by delivery, never seeing other human beings in person.

Slavoj Žižek, *Pandemic! Covid-19 Shakes the World*

NO INSIDE WITHOUT OUTSIDE

HAS YOUR FEELING OF HOME CHANGED SINCE COVID-19?

☐ **YES** ☐ **NO**

MOTIVATE _____

People who spend a long time abroad feel at home again as soon as they board a KLM plane.
KLM knows this.

KLM advertisement

HOW DO YOU COME HOME?

Banners with the text 'Welcome Home', which one sees occasionally, seem rather contrived. It's too much of a good thing. One may welcome strangers and guests, but it doesn't seem quite appropriate for someone who is coming home. Coming home is like taking place in the everyday thread mill; trimmings only make it harder, as they turn something that should be ordinary into some sort of special occasion. If you wish to get to know people, you should get to know them in their daily activities and not focus on those moments in which they explicitly reflect on those activities.

Pieter Hoexum, 'Thuiskomen', archined.nl

DO YOU FEEL AT HOME EVERYWHERE?

Devouriant, *In Muddy Waters*, 2014, deviantart.com

Feeling at home is no longer seen as being rooted in one specific place, as being attached to a certain neighbourhood or town, but as a station along the way, typical of modern dynamic life, or in the refugee camp, waiting for better times:

NOT ROOTS BUT ROUTES

Revolutions in the field of gender as well as globalization bring many changes for people and their feeling of home. We are the architects of our own body and because of emigration and mobility our house can always be somewhere else and the 'home feeling' moves with us. People, commodities, and animals that move with us help this home feeling, as do Starbucks, Apple Stores, and familiar supermarkets. For mobile people these often detested, ubiquitous chains are a great help in developing a home feeling time and again.

Adapted source: Jan Willem Duyvendak, 'Thuis in verandering', nemokennislink.nl

HOME SEEKING?

It's as if the whole world is looking for a 'home'. It is a very topical issue. 'We live in times of collective uprooting — is a feeling shared by many. In politics this sentiment is exploited by right-wing populists in an appalling way.' The political world order falters, never before were so many people displaced or on the run, and for many people globalization comes with uncertainty about their jobs and future. 'Heimat' is back on the political agenda. 'Of course, one can find a home in a region or nation. Still, it is very important to realize that in every society there are people of different cultures, sexual identities, and political affiliations. It is impossible to express all this in a shared cultural identity. Home is not something objective, you cannot answer that question "what is home" for someone else.' 'Home can be good enough, even if it's not an ideal place.' There will always be fantasies about better places.

Ward Janssen

WHERE ARE YOU FROM?

DO YOU FEEL AT HOME AT THE HOME PAGE OF A WEBSITE?

ARE YOU LIVING IN A METAPHOR?

ARE YOU AT HOME IN YOURSELF?

YOUR BODY YOUR HOUSE YOUR CITY
YOUR COUNTRY YOUR OWN LANGUAGE HABITS

TRADITIONS HISTORY

THEY ARE THE INGREDIENTS OF A HOME FEELING

WHERE OR WHEN ARE YOU AT HOME?

☐ In your house, because _____

☐ In your thoughts, because _____

☐ When you're alone, because _____

☐ In your body, because _____

☐ When you're running, because _____

☐ While reading a good book, because _____

☐ With your cat (or dog), because _____

☐ When you're traveling, because _____

☐ Other, because _____

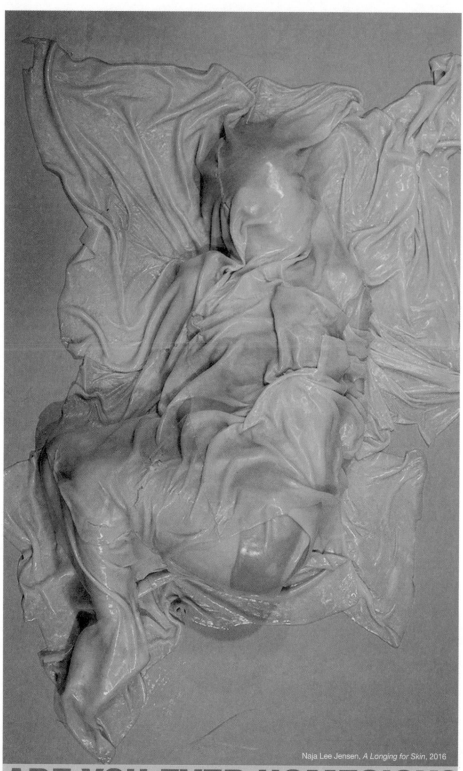

Naja Lee Jensen, *A Longing for Skin*, 2016

ARE YOU EVER HOMESICK?

DRAW YOUR WAY HOME.

USE THE ENTIRE FIELD FOR TEXT AND EXPLANATION.

START HERE

HOME

WHERE ARE YOU?

MOBILITY

ARE YOU A WORLD CITIZEN?

- FREE AND ALWAYS ON THE ROAD?
- YOU WANT TO FLY LIKE A BIRD.
- TO YOU, LOCATIONS ARE UNLIMITED.
- YOU REFUSE TO BE TIED DOWN IN ONE METROPOLE.
- YOU LIVE IN CYBERSPACE.
- YOU ARE OF A NEW CLASS.
- YOUR COMMUNITY IS WIRELESS QUEER.
- YOU FEEL AT HOME EVERYWHERE.
- YOU ARE DATA.
- YOU ARE LIVING WITH YOUR SMARTPHONE, AND SO ALSO WITH UBER AND AIRBNB.
- NETFLIX IS YOUR INTERNATIONAL CUDDLY TOY.
- YOUR LAPTOP IS YOUR OFFICE.
- YOU ARE NOT A CITIZEN, NOT A TOURIST, NOT AN EMPLOYEE.
- YOU ARE THERE ALWAYS AND FOR EVERYONE, 24/7.

I don't think the human race will survive the next thousand years, unless we spread into space.

Stephen Hawking, speaking at the Oxford Union, 14 November 2016

WOULD YOU LIKE TO GO TO MARS?

☐ YES ☐ NO

On your smart phone you visit foreign countries and let yourself be inspired by other cultures. The world in your pocket. The convenience of digital touring makes it logical for us to imagine we will be able to travel to Mars. No destination is too far and everything is possible. But do you really believe this? Are you going to Mars? Mieke Gerritzen

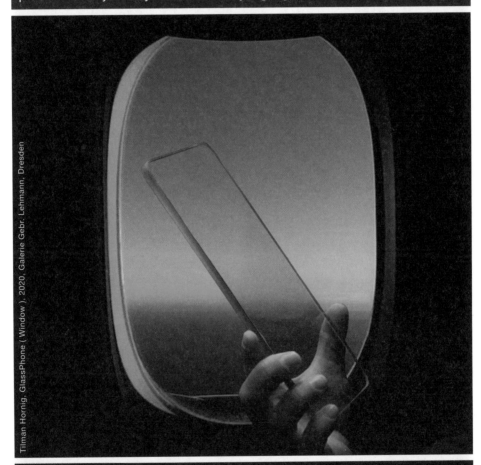

Tilman Hornig, GlassPhone (Window), 2020, Galerie Gebr. Lehmann, Dresden

I'm surprised to see people get so wildly excited about a possible bacterium on Mars when our own planet is crawling with undiscovered species.

George Schaller, *Awake! Magazine*

Hong Kong Central Station, 3 February 2020

YOUR MOBILE MICROBES

Being herd animals, we have structured our society so super mobile over the past decades that we are connected always and everywhere. This makes it difficult to evade a contagious virus. We are social beings. As a species we are not so very different from sheep or ants, from a biological angle. A virus even confronts us with our presence as a collection of cells that stick together and multiply. Our society is a finely-woven network of systems in which not only machines, but also humans are still needed at all levels to make it function. A virus painfully confronts us with issues such as 'equality'. No one, be they white, black, poor, rich, Muslim, or atheist, has any defence against a virus. Microbes do not discriminate; they do not recognize class differences. A virus does not distinguish between friends, family, or strangers. Measures such as keeping distance, quarantine, and isolation are at odds with our nature. Isolation can have serious effects on our psyche. Feelings of boredom, stress, depression, loneliness, powerlessness, and apathy may occur.

https://moneypenny.nl/het-nieuwe-werken/digital-nomads-wfas-remote-workers-thuiswerkers-zie-jij-door-de-bomen-het-bos-nog/

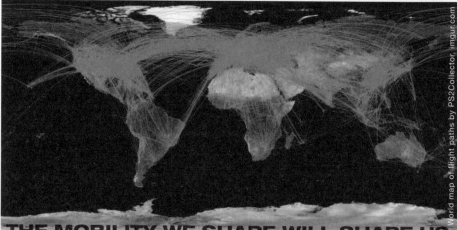

World map of flight paths by PS2Collector, imgur.com

THE MOBILITY WE SHAPE WILL SHAPE US
ARE YOU ALREADY ASHAMED OF FLYING?

HOW DO YOU MOVE TOWARDS THE FUTURE?

☐ By migrating. It is now still a burden, but it will become a choice that many will make. Because society is insecure and overpopulated, you become more mobile and no longer want to have a permanent place of residence. You get rid of all your stuff, become detached and live like a migrant and nomad. You are not afraid of the unknown. Your permanent place is the data stream.

☐ On the electric autoped. Built for world citizens with courage, with the emphasis on exclusivity, speed, stamina under any circumstances, in all kinds of places and with a high fun factor. Suitable for recreation but also for commuters with guts.

☐ Other.

Image: unknown

ARE YOU A SUSTAINABLE WORLD CITIZEN?

SUPER SOLO CULTURE

In the United States, more than one in four people now lives alone; in some parts of the country, especially big cities, that percentage is much higher. You can live alone without being lonely, and you can be lonely without living alone, but the two are closely tied together, which makes lockdowns, sheltering in place, that much harder to bear. Loneliness, it seems unnecessary to say, is terrible for your health. In 2017 and 2018, the former U.S. Surgeon General Vivek H. Murthy declared an 'epidemic of loneliness', and the U.K. appointed a Minister of Loneliness. To diagnose this condition, doctors at U.C.L.A. devised a Loneliness Scale. Do you often, sometimes, rarely, or never feel these ways: I am unhappy doing so many things alone.

I have nobody to talk to. I cannot tolerate being so alone. I feel as if nobody really understands me. I am no longer close to anyone. There is no one I can turn to. I feel isolated from others. In the age of quarantine, does one disease produce another?

Jill Lepore, 'The History of Loneliness', newyorker.com

Renée Zellweger as Bridget Jones, credit: Nicholas Andrew

DO YOU FEEL LONELY DURING A LOCKDOWN?

☐ YES ☐ NO

MOTIVATE _____

WHAT IS YOUR ROUTE?
Place dots and draw lines and explain how and why you were or are there.

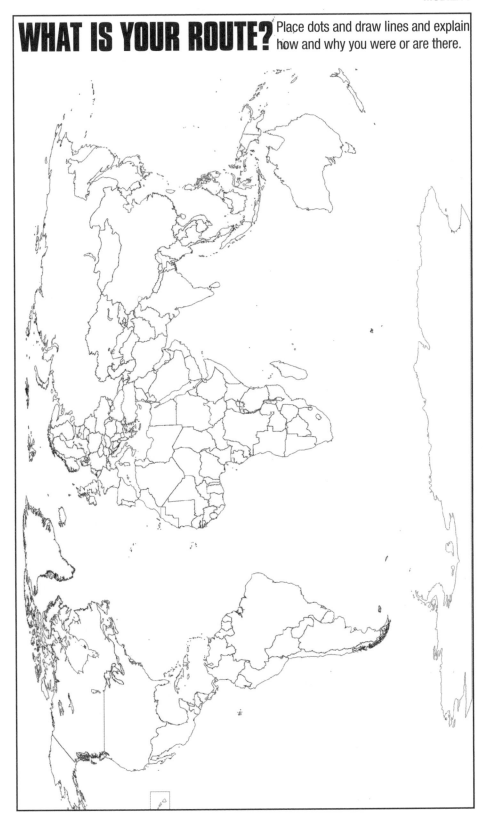

ARE YOU A PRODUCT?

CONSUMING

DO YOU MARKET YOURSELF?

ARE YOU FOR SALE?

ARE YOU DRESSED AS A BILLBOARD?

IS CONSUMUNG A MORAL ACT?

DOES THE LABEL 'NEW' ENTICE YOU?

DO YOU ALWAYS BUY THE SAME?

FOREVER SALE

DO YOU BEGIN TO LIKE THINGS YOU OFTEN SEE?

IS YOUR DESIRE TO BUY CONTROLLED BY ALGORITHMS?

ARE YOU A VICTIM OF THE SYSTEM?

ARE YOU DONE WITH SHOPPING?

PAYING WITH YOUR BODY WILL BECOME QUITE COMMON.

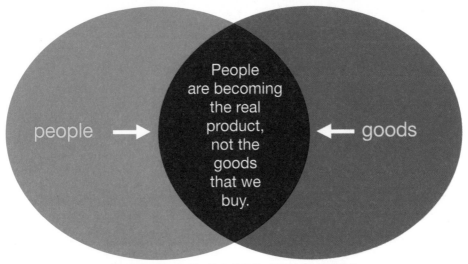

people → People are becoming the real product, not the goods that we buy. ← goods

PEOPLE AND GOODS ARE FUSING.

How do you feel now that you are a consumer product yourself?

☐ **VALUABLE**   ☐ **REDUNDANT**
☐ **AN EXHIBIT**   ☐ **A TOY**
☐ **DATA**   ☐ **STUPID**
☐ **LIKE I BELONG** ☐ **NORMAL**

In China it is generally accepted that cameras record your face for recognition purposes every few metres. Chinese consumers have absolutely no problem with paying with a selfie or logging in by having their faces scanned. Today, these cameras can even read their emotions: companies, and the government too, really know everything about them, even at what moments they are in the mood for special offers. Soon they will be able to read your inside, because when you wear a body tracker you give brands, companies and sometimes even the government access to data about what is going on inside your body.

Pauline Neerman, 'De mens wordt het product in retail', retaildetail.nl

You need to have an image, make a promise and fulfil a promise, you must be predictable. You want to be hired, booked, desired, admired, wanted, bought, paid for, compromised.

Maxim Februari , 'Als de mens een product is, kun je dat ook uitzetten', *NRC Handelsblad*

Dozens of Brazilians reach for television sets in a store in São Paulo. Photo: EPA

HOMO CONSUMERICUS

This is how contemporary man is described, according to the French sociologist Gilles Lipovetsky.

top:
I shop therefore I am, Barbara Kruger's critical slogan from 1978, still topical

left:
Dax Ward, *The abandoned New World Mall, Bankok, Thailand,* daxward.com

HOW MUCH DO YOU SPEND ON DAYS LIKE THIS:

$¥ £€ ◻ **SUPER SATURDAY**
$¥ £€ ◻ **BLACK FRIDAY**
$¥ £€ ◻ **CYBER MONDAY**
$¥ £€ ◻ **SINGLES DAY**
$¥ £€ ◻ **MOTHERS DAY**
$¥ £€ ◻ **FATHERSDAY**
$¥ £€ ◻ **VALENTINE'S DAY**

WHAT IS YOUR ANSWER TO OVER-CONSUMPTION?

HOW OBSESSIVE ARE YOU ABOUT:

	NOT	A LITTLE	VERY
CONSUMING LESS	◻	◻	◻
BEHAVIOURAL THERAPY	◻	◻	◻
NEW DEVELOPMENTS	◻	◻	◻
SUSTAINABILITY	◻	◻	◻
FUTURE SCENARIOS	◻	◻	◻
CHANGE CULTURE	◻	◻	◻
JUICE FASTING	◻	◻	◻
DESIGN THINKING	◻	◻	◻
CIRCULAR ECONOMY	◻	◻	◻

GLOBALLY WE ARE CONSUMING MORE AND MORE VIEWS AND CONCEPTS ABOUT THE SOCIETY WE LIVE IN.
Our appetite for new ideas is infinite.

You are living in a hyper-consumer society that leaves a deep and large ecological footprint. Buying many products, the need to own things, is bad for both mankind and the environment. What can you do about it?

Studium Generale, 'Kritiek consumptiemaatschappij is van alle tijden', sg.uu.nl

CONSUMING LESS?
HERE YOU GO!

We eat everything we see. If you just start eating all kinds of animals, you run a higher risk of being contaminated with an animal virus. If people in the West would eat 30 percent less each day it would save far more lives than can be achieved by fighting the virus. In that sense the virus exposes something: our excessive consuming and our joyriding across the globe. We travel over the world every day by the millions, taking this virus with us. We can't blame the virus for this, we should blame our own behaviour. The virus is forcing us to take a different view on all this. 'The crisis of the COVID-19 virus has the DNA of our modern way of living: consumerism, globalization, mediatization, individualization, technocratization, and a secret longing for lost sacrality.'

Wouter van Noort, 'Damiaan Denys: "Dit virus stelt ons mateloze consumeren aan de kaak"', *NRC Handelsblad*

WE BUY THINGS WE DON'T NEED WITH MONEY WE DON'T HAVE TO IMPRESS PEOPLE WE DON'T LIKE.

Tyler Durden in *The Fight Club*, 1999

CONSUMING LESS IS AN ART.

Consuming less is better for our planet, and it is better for yourself. Materialism, after all, doesn't make one happy. Having less stuff means having more free time, more happiness, and more freedom.

Consuming less is a creative process of awareness.

YOU ARE A LINK IN THE ECONOMIC SYSTEM

WHO ARE YOU?

YOU ARE A LINK IN THE ECONOMIC SYSTEM

1. Low-standard shopping avoiders. Mostly young man who don't see the use for an extensive search on the basis of product qualities. They don't want to spend too much time shopping and more often go for the first acceptable option.

2. Impulsive Hedonics. Mostly young women who like to go shopping and often make impulsive purchases. They love to follow trends and prefer to buy at low prices or a nice discount.

3. Balanced Comparison Shoppers. Relatively older, self-assured consumers who enjoy making extensive comparisons between products and their qualities to eventually buy the best one.

4. Insecure Brand Loyals Mostly younger, slightly lower-educated people who are curious about new products. On the other hand, they often feel overwhelmed and insecure during shopping making them choose well-known brands or seeking the advice of others.

5. Recreational Brand Seekers Mostly older, self-assured women who often buy well-known (expensive and high-quality) brands and care less about the price of products.

6. Task Oriented Shoppers. Mostly older men who don't like the activity of shopping. They are prepared — to an extent — to spend time on it in order to make a better product choice (as opposed to the low demands of the first group).

7. Visionary Scouter People between the ages of 20 and 60 who consume visions and concepts. Writers, thinkers, and philosophers are having the time of their lives. Never before has the future been so popular. This has to do with the non-stop developments in technology.

8. Online Shopping Addict People of all ages buy online. Going to shops is less popular, also because of COVID-19. Online shopping is so easy, and therefore addictive. Some people even order a single bottle of shampoo. This is delivered at your door by car.

9. Activist Shopper You don't buy anything. You don't approve of shopping. You hate money, possessions and anybody and anything that wants to make money. You protest against economic growth. You have a message, but you don't welcome messengers.

Adapted source: 'Consumententypen: welk type shopper ben jij?', centerdata.nl

WHAT DO YOU LEARN FROM DOING NOTHING?

BOREDOM

DOING NOTHING IS DIFFERENT FROM HAVING NOTHING TO DO

Douglas Coupland

WHEN WE ARE BORED, THINGS DON'T MOVE US (ANY LONGER) NOR DO WE MOVE THINGS.

Awee Prins, *Uit verveling*

WHAT IS A THING?

DO YOU DO THINGS? ◯ YES ◯ NO

Things are there to explore, to enjoy, to use until they are no longer of use and can be thrown away.

Awee Prins, *Uit verveling*

DO YOU THINK IT'S DECADENT TO FIND 'DOING NOTHING' OKAY IN A WORLD WHERE SO MUCH STILL NEEDS TO BE DONE?

☐ Yes, because I'm old-fashioned and think you should make good use of your time.

☐ No, because I think that as human beings we must reflect on abundance.

ABOUT BOREDOM

In the late sixties, Susan Sontag wrote in her diary about the 'usefulness of boredom'. When you're bored, says Sontag, you are in a 'stuck mode of attention'. You're looking at the situation from a certain frame and this frame tells you that it is a boring situation. But what if you try another frame of attention? For example, listening rather than looking? Or not looking for meaning but taking the situation as it is? Sontag is daring you to put the blame for the boredom on yourself. It is not the situation; it's how you interpret it. By being aware of that you can find new forms of attention. So, instead of filling a lost moment with Facebook or Twitter, you could try to be aware of the beauty of this so-called lost moment. Ernst-Jan Pfauth, 'Goed voornemen: Durf eens wat vaker niets te doen', decorrespondent.nl

> I think boredom is the beginning of every authentic act. Boredom opens up the space for new engagements. Without boredom, no creativity. If you are not bored, you just stupidly enjoy the situation in which you are.
>
> Slavoj Žižek

It is a modern notion that in the future boredom may become a necessary drug, either by prescription or not. Our society is all about productivity, happiness, and efficiency, which gives being bored a negative connotation and that is pretty old-fashioned. So, from now on being bored is part of finding and recharging yourself. Being consciously bored can be an antidote for overconsumption, as overconsumption is a form of unconscious boredom. The best example of this is, without a doubt, infinite scrolling, this endless scrolling down on the Internet hoping to find something interesting, something new, or whatever. At those moments we are complete outsiders at everything we browse while scrolling: half reading and half understanding to half absorb what we see. It's comparable to people who go shopping out of boredom.

Ward Janssen

CONSUMING OUT OF BOREDOM

In his 1989 book *The Lost Continent* Bill Bryson paints an accurate but poignant picture of how we currently deal with things. 'And as for American closets, they seem to be always full with yesterday's enthusiasms. Golf clubs, scuba diving equipment, tennis rackets, exercise machines, tape recorders, darkroom equipment, objects that once excited their owner and then were replaced by other objects even more shiny and exciting. That is the great, seductive thing about America-the people always get what they want, right now.' If Americans would suddenly run out of closet space, the world would disintegrate.

Awee Prins, *Uit verveling*

TO INCREASE AFFLUENCE, IS TO INCREASE BOREDOM.

Awee Prins, *Uit verveling*

SLOW

The word 'Slow' speaks of a different tempo, conjuring up a sense of spaciousness and possibility, and a richer, deeper experience of life. Its appeal stems from a growing awareness that the speed of contemporary life is propelling humans and the planet down a precarious, disconnected, and unsustainable path. 'Slow' is intended not only to encourage other paces of engagement, but also to inspire the pursuit of more holistic ways of knowing oneself, encountering others, sharing knowledge, and evolving together toward harmonious and resilient forms of living.

Carolyn Strauss, *Slow Reader*

The march of the human mind is slow.

Edmund Burke, *Speech on Conciliation with the Colonies*

WHAT CAN WE LEARN FROM YOUR CAT?

YOU SHOULD START TAKING BOREDOM SERIOUSLY

BOREDOM IS OFTEN A QUESTION OF LONELINESS

FOMO FEAR OF MISSING OUT

STOP INFINITE SCROLLING ON YOUR SMARTPHONE. YOU'RE NOT MISSING ANYTHING!

THE ENDLESS REPETITION

Albert Camus describes the function of endless repetition — actually the most senseless form of boredom — in his 1942 essay 'The Myth of Sisyphus'. The Gods had condemned Sisyphus to the eternal task of pushing a rock up a mountain, and then the rock would roll down and he'd have to start all over again. The intention of this absurd task, a dead-end existence in which your only activity turns out to be useless, time and again, is obvious: punishment. However, according to Camus the despair experienced by Sisyphus was a sign of human dignity, of hope, because he had to experience each setback again, could distance himself from his cursed life and thereby transcend it in a dignified manner. If you wish to actively be bored it's a good idea to look for a 'bore tool' that has some connection to childhood, to actively distance yourself from anything that seems too productive and still belongs to your ordinary life. The most disenchanting example of this perhaps is the colouring book for adults.

Ward Janssen

IF YOU DON'T KNOW WHAT TO DO, CREATE A NEW SELF.

COLOURING BOOK FOR ADULTS →

ARE YOU ALONE WHEN YOU SLEEP?

TO SLEEP

HOW DO YOU SLEEP?

- **DEEP**
- bad
- LIGHT
- **ALONE**
- LIKE A BABY
- WITH PILLS
- **SNORING**
- GOOD

BESIDE YOUR SMARTPHONE

HOW DO YOU FALL ASLEEP?

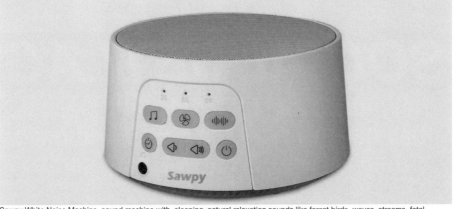

Sawpy White Noise Machine, sound machine with sleeping natural relaxation sounds like forest birds, waves, streams, fetal sounds, lullaby, crickets, thunder, bonfire, seagull, train, hush, dripping.

HOW OFTEN HAVE YOU TRIED COUNTING UNTIL YOU FELL ASLEEP?
☐1X☐2X☐3X☐4X☐5X☐6X☐7X☐8X☐9X☐10X

MAN CHANGES AND SLEEPING ALSO CHANGES.

BUT FOR MANY SLEEPING IS ALSO A PROBLEM.

EVERY NIGHT MILLIONS OF PEOPLE ARE WAITING FOR SLEEP TO COME. SOMETIMES THEY ROAM THEIR DARK HOUSES HALF OR FULLY AWAKE

YOU SLEEP BETTER AFTER AN ORGASM.

According to a recent study about sex as sleep therapy, more than 60 percent of all people experience a higher quality of sleep after they've had an orgasm. It is a fact that the 'happiness substances' that are released are in any case good for your mental rest and night rest. So, better sleep after sex is more fact than fable.

Kiara Louis, 'Beter slapen na de seks: feit of fabel?', bedrock.nl

'FIRST GO TO BED WITH HER, I THOUGHT.
FIRST GO TO BED WITH HER AND THEN TALK.'

WHAT IS BEGUN IN THE FLESH, IS FULFILLED IN THE SPIRIT.

Jan Wolkers, 'Kunstfruit'

IN THE 24-HOUR ECONOMY THERE IS NO TIME TO REST.

SOCIAL JETLAG

Nowadays most people can't sleep if they haven't read the news. And once they've read the news, they can't sleep anymore.

Cees Buddingh

DO YOU LIKE TAKING AN AFTERNOON NAP (INEMURI)?

In Japan sleeping in public is not embarrassing. It's called inemuri and it is a completely accepted phenomenon.

TIPS FOR *INEMURI*:

Do not make a bed under your desk but sleep with your head on the desktop. Don't bring a pillow, but lie your head on your bag (this also keeps you from getting robbed on the train). Do not lean against a perfect stranger while sleeping. Do not snore, it's not polite. While travelling, set a GPS alarm (in your headphones, of course) so that you will awake at the right station.

Nike and Google are experimenting with 'nap pods' (tiny rooms where tired colleagues can take a nap) and flexible office hours for the different biorhythms of morning people and night owls.

I LIKE MY BED MORE THAN I LIKE BIENNALES

I LIKE MY BED MORE THAN I LIKE INTERVIEWS

I LIKE MY BED MORE THAN I LIKE OPEN STUDIOS

I LIKE MY BED MORE THAN I LIKE ART FAIRS

I LIKE MY BED MORE THAN I LIKE EXHIBITION OPENINGS

I LIKE MY BED MORE THAN I LIKE FILM SCREENINGS

I LIKE MY BED MORE THAN I LIKE FESTIVALS

I LIKE MY BED MORE THAN I LIKE LECTURES

I LIKE MY BED MORE THAN I LIKE RESIDENCIES

Source: Eden Mitsenmacher

SLEEP INDUSTRY.

We sleep alone, but later it often turns out that Apple or Google were there while you were sleeping. And depending on the hours of deep sleep you had these companies determine whether you need more new stuff. The American giant manufacturer of luxury mattresses Casper no longer calls itself a 'bed store' but a 'sleep innovator', with a team of 'sleep technicians'. 'We put our best foam forward' is the corporate slogan. Their flagship mattress (the Casper) is responsible for 1,213,446,201 dreams dreamed. And in the small print: 'This number has been estimated based on global sales since 1/1/2017'.

SLEEPING IS TO BE ALONE.

In our sleep we are alone, alone with our dreams and perhaps with our subconscious. But are we really welcome to this moment of being alone? Since Freud's *Die Traumdeutung* (1899) dreaming can be regarded as our primary reaction to the big world outside. In deep sleep we process reality.

HEADSPACE®

DREAMING MOLLIFIES PAINFUL MEMORIES AND CREATES A VIRTUAL REALITY SPACE IN WHICH THE BRAIN MELDS PAST AND PRESENT KNOWLEDGE TO INSPIRE CREATIVITY.

Matthew Walker, *Why We Sleep*

SLEEPING IS PROCESSING.

Sleeping at night was necessary when we did yet not have artificial light and we had to live by daylight. Thomas Edison hated the night time as it prevented him from working and so he invented the incandescent lamp.

The evolution of man shows how we change; maybe it's time to adapt our sleeping habits.

RELAX THE MUSCLES IN YOUR FACE, YOUR TONGUE, YOUR JAW AND EYES. → → → → LET YOUR SHOULDERS DROP AS FAR AS YOU CAN. → → RELAX THE MUSCLES IN YOUR UPPER RIGHT ARM, THEN IN YOUR LOWER ARM. DO THE SAME WITH YOUR LEFT ARM. →BREATHE OUT AND RELAX YOUR CHEST. → → → →RE-LAX THE MUSCLES IN YOUR LEGS, START AT THE TOP OF YOUR THIGHS AND MOVE DOWN.→ → → → →SAY TO YOURSELF FOR TEN SECONDS → →(IN YOUR MIND) 'DON'T THINK',→ → →'DON'T THINK', 'DON'T THINK'.→ →KEEP THIS UP FOR AT LEAST SIX WEEKS GOOD NIGHT!

Traditional sleeping technique in the US Army as described in *Relax and Win. Championship Performance*

ARE YOU PRESENT?

MINDFULNESS

- CONTROL
- OPENNESS
- BALANCE
- OPENNESS
- RHYTHM
- WAVES
- CURRENT
- CIRCULATION
- VOID
- SENSATION
- CONCENTRATION
- FOCUS
- ENERGY
- ATTENTION
- BREATHING
- POWER

HOW DO YOUR LINES RUN?

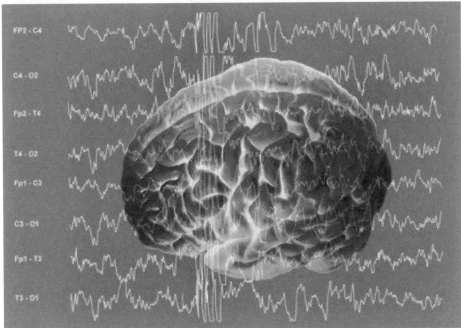

There are five types of brainwaves. They are very much like music notes. Some waves are low frequencies, others are high frequencies. They make sure that your thoughts, emotions, and sensations are nicely balanced.

DELTA THETA ALFA BETA GAMMA

'Hersengolven: delta, thèta, alfa, bèta en gamma', verkenjegeest.com

HAVE YOU TRAINED YOUR BRAINWAVES?

- ○ No, I didn't know I had brainwaves.
- ○ Yes, my brainwaves help me focus my thoughts.
- ○ Not yet, but I would like to experiment with brainwaves.

THE EYE CATCHES...

The brain shapes things.

Paul Cézanne, 'Pensées'

YOU ARE A RIVER!

Life is a stream. A river. You remain static and life moves through you. There's always new water. Doesn't judge, doesn't plan or desire. It just is.

Jelle Hermus. 'Waarom alles in je leven goed is— en waarom het altijd mooi weer is', sochicken.nl

LIVE LIKE WATER

Rivers do not choose their own path. They effortlessly follow their predestined route. They carry large and small rocks, without complaining. At the source they receive new water, which they lose again at their mouth.

Els van de Schoot, 'Geleide meditatie', commithappiness.nl

Sometimes a stream gently laps, sometimes the water swirls wildly, buffeting the rocks, and then sometimes there is a sea of openness. The river itself does not resist this natural movement. We humans often tend to go against the current. Water symbolizes everything that flows within us: desires, feelings, ideas, thoughts, and emotions. Just like water, emotions are sometimes calm and at other times run high and wild. Emotions need to flow, like water in a river. When there is resistance against an emotion, we are blocking the natural flow in our bodies.

Jan Prins, 'Laat emoties stromen als water', inspirerendleven.nl

Waterfalls, ocean waves, and thunderstorms allow our bodies to absorb more oxygen and serotonin; they refresh the mind and stimulate alertness and concentration. Being immersed in water of a natural water source, such as the sea or a lake can also be greatly stimulating for the body. Cold water refreshes both spiritually and physically and has a soothing effect on the nerves, whereas warmer water during the summer can make physical tension disappear. Why looking at water is healthy.

'Waarom kijken naar water gezond is', paradijsvogelsmagazine.nl

DOES YOUR BRAIN GET AN 'ORGASM' FROM ASMR?

 ☐ YES ☐ NO

Autonomous Sensory Meridian Response (ASMR) is a certain sensory sensation that is characterized by a tingling feeling that starts at the back of the head and runs along the neck and back (the sensory meridian response). ASMR is usually experienced as pleasant and soothing and can be evoked by certain visual, auditive, or tactile stimuli, including soft whispering, the creaking of certain objects, the sound or feeling of certain activities (for example, getting a haircut) or seeing someone making a drawing. The experience is also described by some as an 'orgasm of the brain'. Not everyone is equally sensitive to ASMR; some people experience less of the tingling feeling or even don't feel it at all. The experience is therefore not manageable (hence 'autonomous'). ASMR videos: purewow.com/wellness/best-asmr-videos

FROM MEDITATING TO CONSUMING

Is meditation the answer to fifty years of overconsumption? The philosopher Slavoj Žižek once called Buddhism the perfect supplement for the consumer society. Consumers are flexible, nomadic, transnational, eclectic, zapping, and unfaithful. They no longer look for salvation in material things, but in emotional experiences, quality of life, and health. The market of course anticipates these needs by providing wellness centres, medical clinics, biological products, and personal coaching. Emotions, balance, smell, colour, and a 'narrative' become the decisive element in sales.

Source: Marijn Kruk and Pepijn Vloemans, 'Twee Gucci-tassen, pas de problème, maar meer dan dat?', *De Groene Amsterdammer*

WHEREVER YOU GO, THERE YOU ARE.

Jon Kabat-Zinn

HUMANS ARE BASICALLY HABIT MACHINES...
Naval Ravikant

McMindful

Mindfulness is all the rage. It is clear that mindfulness has gone mainstream. Some have even called it a revolution. But what if, instead of changing the world, mindfulness has become a banal form of capitalist spirituality that mindlessly avoids social and political transformation, reinforcing the neoliberal status quo? In McMindfulness, Ronald Purser debunks the so-called mindfulness revolution, exposing how corporations, schools, governments and the military have co-opted it as a technique for social control and self-pacification. Purser busts the myths its salesmen rely on, challenging the narrative that stress is self-imposed and mindfulness is the cure-all. If we are to harness the truly revolutionary potential of mindfulness, we have to cast off its neoliberal shackles, liberating mindfulness for a collective awakening.

Ronald Purser, *McMindfulness: How Mindfulness Became the New Capitalist Spirituality*

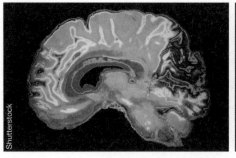
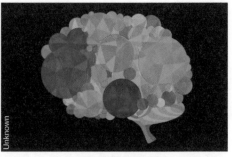

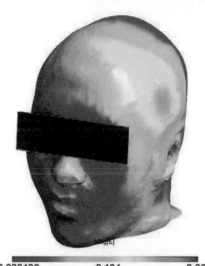
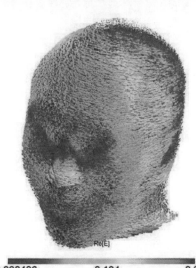

| 0.000406 | 0.184 | 0.367 | 0.000406 | 0.184 | 0.367 |

Electric field induced on the surface of the human head model due to 900 MHz horizontally polarized plane wave (left). Direction of the electric field (right).

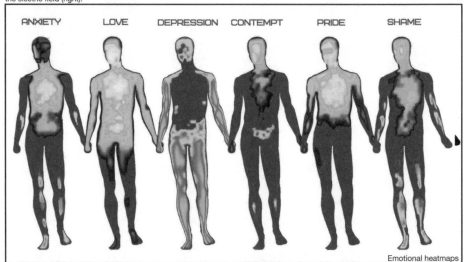

ANXIETY LOVE DEPRESSION CONTEMPT PRIDE SHAME

Emotional heatmaps

VISUALIZE YOUR MOOD

Draw your mood, your emotions on the opposite page.
Use colour and text. Draw your inner and outer world. ⟶

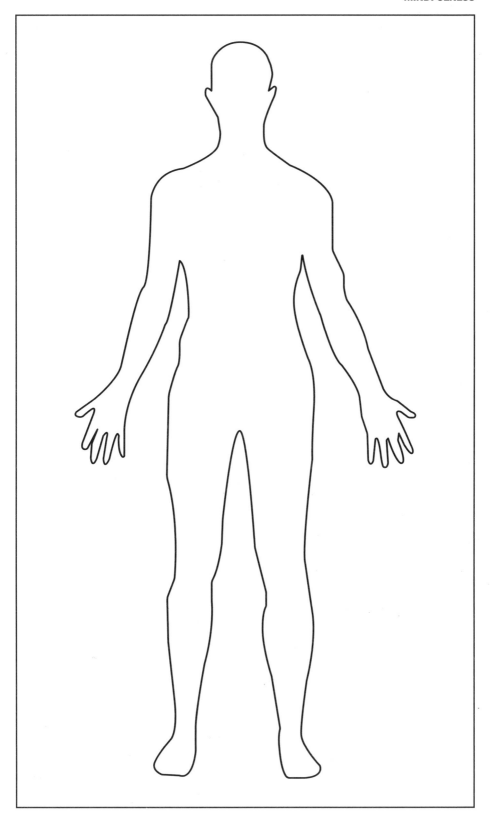

BARTON BIGGS
WEALTH, WAR & WISDOM
WILEY
HOW TO MAKE MONEY
BARNUM, KNOX, AND LIPMAN
A COMPLETE GUIDE TO BUILDING WEALTH
HOW TO GET RICH
Felix Dennis
THE ELEMENTS OF INVESTING
CHARLES D. ELLIS
BURTON G. MALKIEL
WEALTH SECRETS
How the Rich Got Rich
SAM WILKIN
LIVING WITH WEALTH WITHOUT LOSING YOUR SOUL
STEVE PERRY
YOU ARE A BADASS AT MAKING MONEY
JEN SINCERO
13 STEPS TO BLOODY GOOD WEALTH
ASHWIN SANGHI
SUNIL DALAL
THE TRUTH ABOUT KEEPING SECRETS
Keys to Guaranteed Biblical WEALTH & PROSPERITY
CelebratingFinancialFreedom.com
eBook Media Viewer
THINK AND GROW RICH
ORIGINAL CLASSIC VERSION
NAPOLEON HILL
I AM RICH
the only thing you need to know
J. Pauls
I WILL TEACH YOU TO BE RICH
RAMIT SETHI
No Guilt. No Excuses. No B.S. Just a 6-Week Program That Works.
THE WEALTH MINDSET
NEVILLE GODDARD
make money LIVE WEALTHY
MONEY IS YOUR FRIEND

DO YOU ENRICH YOURSELF?

WEALTH

DO YOU LIVE IN POVERTY WHILE YOU HAVE ENOUGH MONEY?

WEALTH IS A MATTER OF DRAWING THE LINES.

CONSUME CRITICALLY!

Stock market bubbles don't grow out of thin air. They have a solid basis in reality, but reality as distorted by a misconception.

George Soros

ARE YOU IN FAVOUR OF A BASIC INCOME FOR EVERYONE?

☐ YES ☐ NO

WHY?_____

HAS THE TIME FINALLY COME FOR UNIVERSAL BASIC INCOME?

FREE MONEY WORKS!

Rutger Bregman, *Utopia for Realists*

MONEY IS JUST A MEANS OF EXCHANGE

Douglas Rushkoff, https://rushkoff.com/books/team-human-book

HOW RICH ARE YOU?

 COLOUR THE BARS

MONEY

POOR	RICH

SATISFACTION

POOR	RICH

LOVE

POOR	RICH

Breathe in. Your lungs are filled with oxygen. Breathe out. Now they are almost completely empty again. Not to worry. You know that soon they will be filled with fresh air again. There is no point in sucking as much oxygen as you can into your lungs and then hold your breath. Air must circulate, or you will suffocate. You can also look at wealth in this way. For many people wealth is the same thing as having a lot of money. But money is not there to make us rich. It is just a means of exchange, allowing us to exchange goods in a convenient manner: I breed chickens, you make shoes. I want a pair of shoes from you, but you are not interested in chickens. So, I give you money instead of chickens. It's a simple as that. The intention has never been to collect this convenient means of exchange in a big bag and hang onto it for dear life. No, money has to circulate, just like air.

IT'S NOT ABOUT WHAT YOU HAVE, BUT WHAT YOU DO.

'It helps if you look at wealth not as a number on your bank statement but as the value that you exchange with other people. Wealth is not something that you have, it's something that you do. Something that someone else is willing to pay for, and vice versa. Money then flows in and out by itself. The result, eventually, is a healthier economic system. You create a sustainable seed-bed for the benefit of all. An orchard where everyone can always pick fruit, instead of having only a single full fridge only for yourself.'

IF YOU WANT TO BE RICH, YOU SHOULD MAKE OTHER PEOPLE RICH.

'As long as there are huge differences between people there will always be others who have their eye on your wealth. Only in a world where everyone experiences wealth are you truly safe.'

And feeling safe is exactly what we want. It is the main reason why people want to be rich. The more money you have, the safer you are, they think. But what if you would not put a price on that safety but simply ask yourself: in what situation would I feel comfortable? Often that feeling comes from quite different things than material possessions. A nice neighbour who lends you his lawnmower. A friendly baker who gives you an extra free roll because you are a regular customer. That student in your street who helps your child with math once in a while. These are all things that are not directly related to money but that are very valuable. Do the shopping for someone else sometimes, organize a barbecue for the neighbourhood, repair a puncture for the girl next door. That way you don't need a million in your bank account and still be incredibly rich.'

'Kijk anders naar rijkdom: 3 tips van filosoof Douglas Rushkoff', dekleurvangeld.nl

ARE YOU IN FAVOUR OF MORE EQUALITY AND SPREADING OF MONEY?

YES ☐   NO ☐

MOTIVATE _____

EVERYBODY RICH?

'If you imagine a world of real abundance. Like a world where we built the right AI that's just pulling wealth out of the atmosphere and no one really has to work anymore, because we literally have machines that can build machines that can build machines, that are all powered by sunlight, that do everything better than we can. Now why wouldn't that be some kind of utopia? Well it wouldn't be a utopia because we have these very weird emotions, or many of us do, that make it seem like it would be wrong to spread the wealth around. Most people are living as though they want to live in a world where there's a few trillionaires living in compounds ringed by razor wire, and everyone else is sort of starving to death. It's like a winner take all scenario. And so, we have to find a new ethic whereby people are no longer—their purchase on existence is no longer justified by doing profitable work that other people will pay them for. In a world of true abundance you shouldn't have to work to justify your life. You should be free to enjoy the wealth of the world. If we are going to get to that place, we have to change our ethics around that.'

Sam Harris, goodreads.com/quotes/tag/universal-basic-income

In 2018 Jeff Bezos (founder of Amazon) was the first to reach the 100-billion-dollar mark. That's a figure that most people can't even imagine. Roughly speaking you could say that Bezos has the same amount of money as what 3,225,000 regular citizens together earn in one year.

Ward Janssen

IF YOU'RE IN FAVOUR OF EQUALITY, THEN WHAT'S YOUR TAKE ON THE GAP BETWEEN RICH AND POOR?

More and more money is earned by fewer and fewer people.

PRIVATE PROPERTY MUST BE DISTRIBUTED BETTER AND POSSESSIONS SHOULD BE TEMPORARY.

THOMAS PIKETTY

Just like eating the wrong fats, we should fight bad forms of wealth.

THE WEALTHY COULD PAY MORE TAX FOR A BETTER DISTRIBUTION.

DO YOU THINK ABOUT POVERTY?

'Extreme wealth and poverty go hand in hand because of the unjust distribution of prosperity. Of course, we also have to be concerned about poverty. But that's already being done; scientists and policy-makers think about who should be considered as poor and what causes their poverty. That's why we have a poverty line. Those living below that line don't have enough money and means to sustain themselves. One of the criteria for judging a government's policy is whether the number of people living below the poverty line — people who are officially poor — is decreasing or increasing. So, we have all these questions about poverty, but not about wealth. This is remarkable.'

Ingrid Robeyns in Alexandra van Ditmars, 'Niemand heeft een moreel recht op rijkdom', human.nl

IS YOUR POLITICAL PREFERENCE LINKED TO HOW RICH YOU ARE?

☐ RIGHT ☐ MIDDLE ☐ POOR
☐ LEFT ☐ MIDDLE ☐ RIGHT

LESS THAN 1 PERCENT OF THE WORLD POPULATION OWNS 48 PERCENT OF THE WEALTH ON THE PLANET. THIS GLOBAL ELITE DOESN'T MIND SUPPORTING CHARITIES AS LONG AS THEY FLATTER THEIR VANITY.

Heleen Mees, 'De allerrijksten willen wel geven, maar het liefst aan goede doelen die hun ijdelheid strelen', *de Volkskrant*

The art world is one of the domains of the rich and super-rich. Art collectors build up investment portfolios with exclusive possessions, and market value is more important than the artistic quality of the work. Contemporary art lends itself very well to speculation. Or would you rather speculate on the stock exchange? Ward Janssen

STEP INTO THE SHOES OF A SUPER-RICH. WHAT WOULD YOU DO WITH YOUR MONEY?

Technology ○
You invest in new technology, buy shares and hope their value rises.

Art ○
You invest by buying famous artwork that will probably rise in value.

Private Museum ○
You build a museum for your own collection. This flatters your ego while serving the public. Admission is expensive, though.

Fund ○
You donate every year to support artists.

THE GOLDEN MEAN?

'To Aristotle, the economy was part of ethics. An important element in his ethics was a clear distinction between goals and means. For Aristotle, goals were innate in the nature of animated creatures. Thus, an acorn's goal is to become an oak tree. And the goal of humans is to become good humans, which for Aristotle meant: leading a good life. He also had an answer to the question what that good life would entail: a virtuous life. In his ethics he stresses that it is important to avoid extremes in virtues, i.e. in character traits or attitudes: we must strike the golden mean between too much and too little. In the case of spending money, generosity is a virtue that strikes the golden mean between the vices of avarice — spending far too little — and extravagance: spending far too much.'

Ingrid Robeyns in Alexandra van Ditmars, 'Niemand heeft een moreel recht op rijkdom', human.nl

MONEY IN ITSELF IS NO LONGER A SIGN OF WEALTH, YOU NEED TO HAVE TASTE TO ALSO CREATE STATUS WITH YOUR CAPITAL.

Ward Janssen

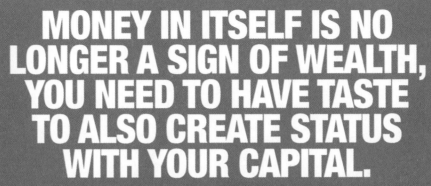

I LIVE IN A LUXURY APARTMENT BUILDING IN ONE OF THE MOST EXPENSIVE AREAS OF D.C

BUT I AM ALWAYS READY TO TELL YOU ABOUT BEING POOR, DESPERATE AND A GOOD SOCIALIST.

Society appreciates outward values such as success, power, prosperity, wealth, physical beauty. And those values are in conflict with inner qualities such as truth, peace, justice, and so on. If you are concerned with outward values you want to be seen, be noticed, be special. Actually, there are only two options. You either strive for prestige, fame, and wealth, which means you seek attention and therefore will experience isolation and discontent. Or you strive for peace and look at how you can mean something to other people, to the world around you, which means you will experience fulfilment. Your ratio will tell you that you don't need to choose, that you can have both the inner values and the outward appearance. Your soul knows that this is a seduction tactic.

Petra van der Horst, 'Innerlijk of uiterlijk?', horstconsult.nl

WHAT DO YOU CHOOSE?

☐ **OUTWARD APPEARANCE** (SUCCESS, POWER, WEALTH, MONEY)

☐ **INNER VALUES** (TRUTH, PEACE, JUSTICE)

BECOME WHO YOU ARE?

CAREER

ARE YOU A CLIMBER?

Are you a 'paper pusher'?

DO YOU HAVE A BULLSHIT JOB?

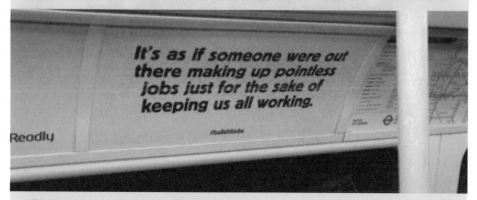

It's as if someone were out there making up pointless jobs just for the sake of keeping us all working.

Readly

Can you build a career on a basic income?

 Sure!
Because, _____

 No, never!
Because, _____

A FLOWER DOES NOT THINK OF COMPETING TO THE FLOWER NEXT TO IT.
It just blooms.

Zen Shin

TAKE ANOTHER STEP SOME-WHERE, ONE MORE TIME.

'It was as if he hadn't finished his sentence: take another step somewhere, one more time before… Before he would begin to sit around, waiting to die? Before some horrible illness would come and consume his body? Before the horsemen of the apocalypse arrived? Before climate change had made life on earth impossible? His remark didn't show any job satisfaction either. As if work was only a vehicle for taking steps.'

Binnert de Beaufort, 'Een carrière als ladder: een essay', *Het Financieele Dagblad*

THE NEXT STEP AS A:

☐ Workhorse ☐ Fancy horse

Because, ——————————— Because, ———————————

WHAT DO YOU WANT TO ACHIEVE?

- STATUS
- FUN
- HEALTH
- MOBILITY
- HOMELINESS
- POWER

- HAPPINESS
- VISION
- A LOT OF MONEY
- ME-TIME
- A NEW LOVE
- SOCIAL CONTEXT

CAREER CHANGE

BE YOU!

BE AWARE!

Bad jobs are bad because they're hard or they have terrible conditions or the pay sucks, but often these jobs are very useful. In fact, in our society, often the more useful the work is, the less they pay you. Whereas bullshit jobs are often highly respected and pay well but are completely pointless, and the people doing them know this.

Sean Illing, 'Bullshit Jobs: Why They Exist and Why You Might Have One', vox.com

FAKE IT UNTIL YOU MAKE IT

Image: unknown

Sure, sitting in a cubicle playing Candy Crush all day is soul-killing—but what else are you gonna do, play Candy Crush all day at home alone?

IS WORK WHAT WILL SAVE YOU, OR WHAT YOU NEED TO BE SAVED FROM?

Jonah Galeota-Sprung, 'Bullshit Jobs', thepointmag.com

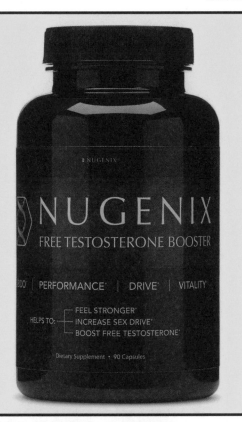

IS TESTOSTERONE THE COMPETITION HORMONE?

Generally speaking, men with a higher social status do have higher testosterone levels, just like the top monkey has among other apes. Testosterone is also related to the will to win. However, there are also many men who although they have a lot of testosterone do not strive for dominance. With them the effect of testosterone is mitigated by a high stress level — cortisol. And there are environments, for example corporate cultures, where dominance is not achieved by competition but by working together. In that case the hormone will stimulate just that. This is because there are two ways to achieve status: via dominance, so by striving for and exercising power, and via prestige. Unlike dominance, prestige is not related to testosterone. Prestige even seems to suppress testosterone. The young researcher with professorship ambitions has nothing to gain by intimidating his esteemed opponent when this opponent poses a complicated question. In short: in a culture where prestige is seen as more important than dominance, that strategy will be used more often; in a harsh, ruthless world the testosterone-based status will prevail. In prison you won't get far by organizing a 'best writer' or 'best darts player' competition to establish the picking order.

Job de Vrieze, 'Dit doet testosteron écht met je gedrag', decorrespondent.nl

> Labour no longer is a matter of savoir-faire (knowing how to do), but a matter of savoir-vivre (knowing how to live).
> Bernard Stiegler

HAVING A CAREER WITHOUT A JOB.

If we can fully design ourselves, the responsibility for not failing is also exclusively our own. But what is failing today? There was a time when collective frameworks defined the status of a career, but nowadays we have to do everything ourselves. Career planning is pointless. There are hardly any jobs with a future. More and more people nowadays are freelancers. If working is no longer the highest goal, structuring your free time as interestingly and effectively as possible becomes the biggest challenge and then you no longer need a job for a glorious career. Then you have to start thinking about what you want to bring to society. Then your career is not about your work, but about whether you are making a meaningful contribution to society.

Sofie Rozendaal, 'Een droom opgeven is geen nederlaag', *NRC Handelsblad*

WHAT DO YOU BRING TO SOCIETY?

- *GAIETY*
- *MISERY*
- *NEW KNOWLEDGE*
- *EXPERTISE*
- *REFLECTION*
- *NOTHING*

WHAT IS YOUR SOCIAL STATUS?

Social status can be the result of 'cultural' types of capital such as being highly educated or having great intellectual prestige. But also practising a difficult and/or important profession (think of professional football players), or being physically attractive. The general belief today is that anyone can reach anything as long as they work hard at it. What you can do and what you choose defines your social position. This allows higher educated people to have a feeling of superiority towards the lower educated and to even regard them as 'less than them'. Through superior — or, rather, arrogant — behaviour with regard to someone's level of education you actually create social inequality, making you co-responsible for the uneven positions among people. It's individual choices, such as engaging in the above-mentioned behaviour, that make people feel unwanted and of less value than others. It's not the differences that create social inequality but the way in which you handle those differences that create the inequality between people.

'Opleiding bepaalt maatschappelijke positie', metronieuws.nl

DO YOU RESPECT WHAT OTHERS DO?

- *Yes, I always bring out the best in people and compliment them.*
- *No, not always. I have high standards and I am often jealous.*

WHAT ARE THE STEPS IN YOUR CAREER?

FILL THE CIRCLES WITH CATCHWORDS, IDEAS, PICTURES OR RULES.

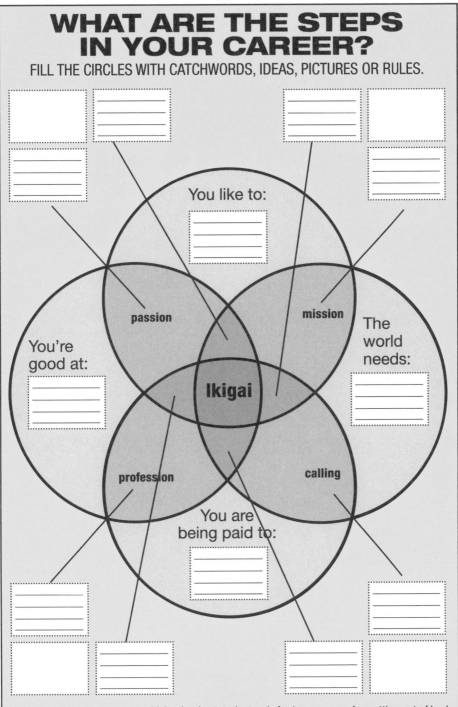

Ikigai is a Japanese concept which, simply stated, stands for 'your reason for getting out of bed in the morning'. In French this is sometimes called 'raison d'être'. Ikigai is a contraction of the words 'iki', meaning life or living, and the word 'kai' (pronounced guy), which stands for value, effect, result, or usefulness. The word *ikigai* refers to having a direction or purpose in life, that which makes one's life worthwhile, and towards which an individual takes spontaneous and willing actions giving them satisfaction and a sense of meaning to life.

ARE YOU AN ART- WORK?

CREATIVITY

DO YOU HAVE A GOOD IDEA?

IDEAS FIGHT EACH OTHER.

HOW TO TURN YOUR CREATIVITY INTO MONEY?

Mieke Gerritzen

ARE YOU PAID TO CREATE?

ARE YOU CREATIVE ON COMMAND? ✓ ✗

BECOME A PLATFORM

DASEIN IS DESIGN

Henk Oosterling, *Radicale middelmatigheid*

CAN YOU THINK LIKE AN ARTIST?

CREATIVITY IS ALL YOU HAVE LEFT

> People degrade themselves in order to make machines seem smart all the time. We have repeatedly demonstrated our species bottomless ability to lower our standards to make information technology look good. Every instance of intelligence in a machine is ambiguous.
>
> Jaron Lanier

WHAT DOES TECHNOLOGY DO TO YOUR CREATIVITY?

'Let's say you check your email fifty times a day, which will take one minute each time. This not only means that you spend almost an hour every day on checking your mail, but also that each time you are interrupted from your work you switch over to your left brain. And this while creativity happens to take place in the right half of your brain. So, people who are constantly busy with their phone cannot simultaneously be calm enough to have creative ideas.'

Chris Lewis in Loeka Oostra, 'Technologie staat creativiteit in de weg', mt.nl

IS CREATIVITY ONLY FUN AS LONG AS IT'S A PROCES?

☐ YES ☐ NO

MOTIVATE _____

> According to Yuval Harari, creativity is everyone's curiosity to build on the history of thoughts, inventions, and facts, on behalf of innovation. This used to be the preserve of artists; now it applies to anyone.
>
> Mieke Gerritzen

DO YOU LOOK AT YOURSELF AS AN ARTWORK?

○ YES, I AM AN ARTWORK THAT IS NEVER FINISHED.
○ NO, I AM HUMAN, YOU CAN'T CHANGE ANYTHING WITH ME.

YOU ARE MAKEABLE
WHICH CREATIVE PROCESS DO YOU ENGAGE WITH ABOUT YOURSELF?

- ☐ **PROGRAMMING**
- ☐ **MANIPULATION**
- ☐ **RE-USE**
- ☐ **UPGRADE**
- ☐ **COMBINING**
- ☐ **COPY-PASTE**
- ☐ **RECOMBINING**
- ☐ **GROWING**

WE ARE ALL BORN ORIGINALS WHY IS IT SO MANY OF US DIE COPIES.

Edward Young

The democratization of technologic has made it possible for anyone to resume or remix somebody else's work. *Copy paste, combine and recombine all you want, add your own inspiration, and free ideas to create evolution and growth.* Copying is perceived as something negative, something non-creative. There is only a network full of inspirations and ideas which can be transformed into something new: creation apparently requires influence. There's no need for protection of an idea, because every idea is a connection in itself.

Sanne van Beek, 'Curated Culture', sannevanderbeek.nl

CREATIVITY COMES FROM A CONFLICT OF IDEAS.

Donatella Versace

On the left: **MANDALA**. For ages, Buddhist monks have been making complex creations in sand patterns: mandalas, in which coloured sand forms geometric mosaics in concentric circles. And after all this, when the creation is finished, they wipe it out with one swift movement of the hand, bringing it back to nothing, to just plain sand. It is all about celebrating creation without a product.

IS THERE A FUTURE FOR YOU AS AN ARTIST?

- ☐ YES, I HAVE MANY FRIENDS IN ART.
- ☐ YES, BECAUSE I'M A LEFTY.
- ☐ YES, I AM CREATIVE WITH GRANTS.
- ☐ YES, I HAVE AN EYE FOR TRENDS.
- ☐ YES, I AM INTO DIVERSITY.
- ☐ YES, I LOOK ARTISTIC.

THINGSAREWHAT YOUMAKEOFTHEM

WHAT ARE YOU DREAMING OF?

TO FLY LIKE A BIRD?

TO LIVE ON THE MOON?

TO SWIM LIKE A DOLPHIN?

TO COMMUNICATE VIA SONAR?

TELEPATHY WITH A LOVER?

EQUALITY BETWEEN SEXES AND RACES?

EMPATHY AS AN EXTRA SENSE?

A HOUSE THAT GROWS WITH YOUR FAMILY?

TO LIVE LONGER?

Koert van Mensvoort, 'Next Nature Network', nextnature.net

THINK	TRY
DISCOVER	GENERATE
INFORM	IMPLEMENT
DEFINE	IMPROVE
STUDY	IMAGINE

ARE YOU CREATIVE?

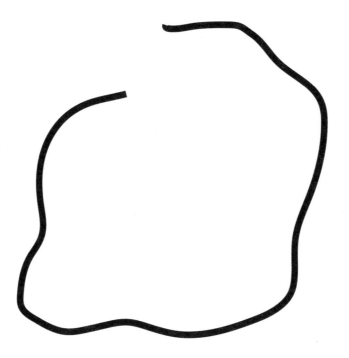

FINISH THIS PICTURE.

Torrance Test Model of Creative Thinking

DO YOU WEAR YOUR BRAIN OUTSIDE YOUR SKULL?

KNOWLEDGE

Who teaches you?

WHAT DO YOU SEE?
WHAT DO YOU READ?
HOW AND WHERE?

Are you a street reader?

OR AN INFO SCAVENGER?

DO YOU WANT TO KNOW EVERYTHING?

ARE YOU ONE OF THE NEW GENERATION OF READERS?
ARE YOU:

- ## KNOWLEDGE WORKER?
- ## KNOWLEDGE KNOWER?

- ## YOU READ.
- ## YOU ARE BEING READ.

KNOW YOURSELF. KNOWLEDGE IS POWER
(Socrates)   **(Bacon, Meditationes Sacrae)**

The more knowledge I absorb, the more I realize how little I know. I know that I know nothing, which makes it seem I know more than others (after Socrates)

THE ONLY SOURCE OF KNOWLEDGE IS EXPERIENCE
Albert Einstein

Still from short film Yellow, 2006, directed by Neil Blomkamp, viral ad for the Adicolor Yellow campaign for Adidas by IDEALOGUE.

HOW FULL OF KNOWLEDGE ARE YOU?

Around 600 BC, Greek philosophers, poets, artists, and other intellectuals had started launching a new idea of mankind. Instead of being insignificant slaves, mankind was assigned a central role. Since time memorial the majority of the population had always been assured that they were in God or in the divine and that 'HE' was infinite. Now, more than 2500 years later, mankind itself has already gathered so much knowledge that it is no longer possible to store all that knowledge in one person. Man is becoming full! Therefore the 'cloud' is a welcome storage space for knowledge and information that the overfull individuals can no longer carry with them. There's no need to remember things, you just look them up. What we are able to know now, is incredibly much. One push of a button and Google and Wikipedia are at our service. We are, as it were, outsourcing the stacking of all this knowledge to an infinitely large memory; not a divine memory, but a virtual one. Mankind itself thus gains a little more space.

Source: geheimenindebijbel.nl; godenenmensen.com

WHERE IS YOUR KNOWLEDGE?

INSIDE YOUR HEAD

OUTSIDE YOUR HEAD

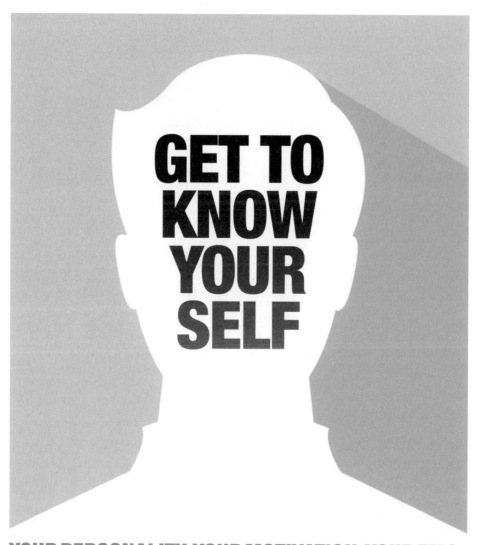

GET TO KNOW YOUR SELF

YOUR PERSONALITY. YOUR MOTIVATION. YOUR EMO-
TIONAL INTELLIGENCE. YOUR SELF-CONFIDENCE.
YOUR FEARS. YOUR HABITS. YOUR CRAVINGS. YOUR
POSSIBILITIES. YOUR LIFESTYLE. YOUR SENSE OF
HUMOR. YOUR 'WHY'. YOUR NATURAL STRENGTHS.
YOUR POLITICAL CHOICE. YOUR HOBBIES AND LIFE
SKILLS. YOUR TALENTS. YOUR PERSONAL LEARN-
ING STYLE. YOUR LIFE EXPERIENCES. YOUR VALUES.
YOUR CAPACITY FOR EMPATHY. YOUR NEGATIVE
THOUGHTS. YOUR ABILITY. YOUR DESIRES. YOUR
EXPECTATIONS. YOUR SELF-AWARENESS PRAC-
TICE. YOUR RISK TOLERANCE. YOUR MISTAKES.

READY TO LEARN ABOUT YOUR SELF?

KNOW YOURSELF

Mankind has always felt itself to be part of the universe and dependent on cosmic forces, but by cultivating our own identity this gradually changed. The divine universe was replaced by universities, knowledge institutes, and research centres that fed human intelligence with knowledge for developing the planet. But have we, amidst this seemingly unlimited freedom and a culture that is characterized by consumption and virtuality, become disoriented and estranged from our being?

René Gude and Ad Verbrugge, *Ken Uzelve*

IS THE KNOWLEDGE THAT YOU HAVE ACCESS TO REALLY YOURS?

☐ YES   ☐ NO

MOTIVATE

SUNSTREAM.TV

#SELFDESIGNACADEMY
LEARNING ABOUT YOUR SELF

The knowledge you accumulate comes from outside. It is knowledge outside of your self. What is missing is knowledge about your self. Self-knowledge. Why is the study of our selves not part of the knowledge we acquire? Why isn't a course in self-knowledge part of the curriculum in schools? Self-knowledge can help us to understand jealousy, revenge, resentment, depression, and fears. Self-knowledge helps you to function more efficiently and enjoy the things you do more. There is no point in being given knowledge by others; you need to experience it yourself. The self-help industry has discovered that there is a great need for self-knowledge and has by now become an economic factor. But self-help, self-coping and self-knowledge really ought to be part of education.

Mieke Gerritzen

IS THERE STILL AN AUTHORITY IN THE FIELD OF KNOWLEDGE OR ARE YOU ON YOUR OWN?

ARE YOU AN INFORMATION FILTER?

☐ YES ☐ NO

ARE YOU LONGING FOR THE NEXT INFORMATION WAVE TO STIMULATE YOUR CREATIVITY?

After thirty years of building it the digital empire is now a databank for the slurping people who are transforming unnoticed and are being reduced to pumping stations of flesh and blood through which data is being pressed to satisfy the information hunger. People as filters. Data are rather ambiguous; on the one hand they are actual information, they are what we know, but on the other hand they seem to be intangible matter that hides itself. Because we cannot observe the cloud directly and therefore can't get a grip on the data that are hiding out there, the whole atmosphere surrounding knowledge becomes somewhat mysterious. Big Data, NSA, Prism, Apple, Amazon, Wikileaks, Google, Facebook and Netflix exert enormous influence on your personal development. Through these suppliers of knowledge, we are creating similar ideas all over the world. Imagine your creative ideas also being thought of on the other side of the world. It is one of mankind's oldest dreams: to collect all knowledge in one place. The library of Alexandria was the first attempt. Google books is the most recent one. Did Google make that old dream come true: all the knowledge for everyone available all the time and anywhere?

Source: radio1.be/alles-altijd-overal-voor-iedereen

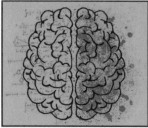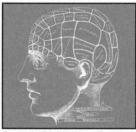

Parc Taulí Neurosciences, tauli.cat

From Luke Dittrich, 'All the President's Neuroscientists', esquire.com

The brain according to Cornel Bierens, cornelbierens.nl

WHERE DO YOU SEARCH?

AND ARE YOU SEARCHING ANONYMOUSLY?

WHERE IS YOUR KNOWLEDGE?

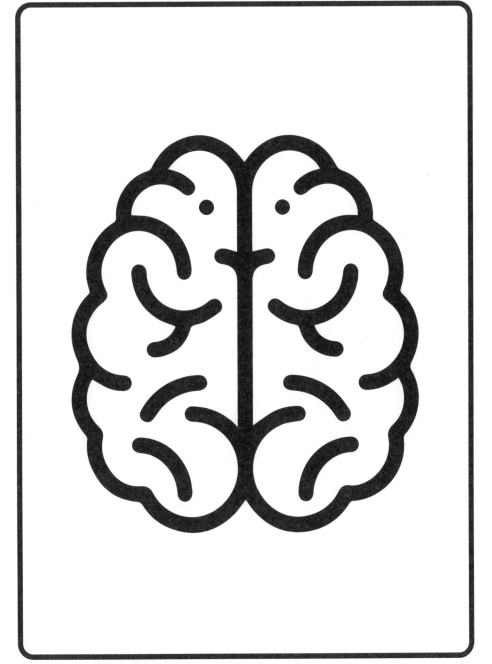

DRAW A FLOOR PLAN OF YOUR KNOWLEDGE WORLD.

Use text and colour. Inside and outside your brain. Visualize as much as you can. See examples of brain images on the previous page.

ARE YOU A SYSTEM ANIMAL?

MANAGEMENT

HOW ORGANIZED ARE YOU?

- ☐ I THINK IN BOXES
- ☐ LIKE A CONTROL FREAK
- ☐ LIKE A BUREAUCRAT
- ☐ DOWDY
- ☐ WITHOUT HIERARCHY
- ☐ CHAOTIC
- ☐ WITH FORESIGHT
- ☐ IMAGINATIVE
- ☐ FROM POWER
- ☐ PROCESS-DRIVEN
- ☐ AS THE NEED ARISES
- ☐ VIA THE SYSTEMS
- ☐ COMPELLING
- ☐ EXPERIMENTAL
- ☐ WITHOUT A PLAN
- ☐ ORGANIC

HAVE YOU BECOME TRAPPED IN THE SYSTEMS?

Us humans have always organized our lives in systems: motorways, sewage networks, electricity grids, cities, governments, corporations, the Internet, the alphabet, capitalism, communism, money, religion. Although systems have brought us much — feeding us, keeping us warm, safe, and healthy — we can also easily become prisoners of our own organizational skills. Do you suffer from choice stress? What will you have for dinner tonight? What clothes will you wear? How can you organize your time effectively? You are probably very busy, you have far too much stuff, you lose things, you are socially overstrung and in spite of all that you keep checking your phone all day long. The smartphone, Internet banking, GPS navigation, they all make our life easier but they also bring an addictive and controlling atmosphere.

Source: Koert van Mensvoort and Mieke Gerritzen, *Save the Humans!*

CREATE THE NEW WORLD ORDER

Piet Mondrian became a famous painter with his abstract works of rectangular planes and straight lines. The geometrically abstract forms emanated a sense of unity and balance, and reflected his need for order and system.

By seeing an organization as an organism, we can study in a different way than before how there is a hierarchy and growing complexity within systems, and how the relation between parts and whole play a role in this.

Ludwig von Bertalanffy, biologist (1901–1972)

HOW DO YOU WISH TO LIVE?

MASLOW'S PYRAMID

Abraham Maslow, an American psychotherapist and founder of the humanist school in psychology, developed a world-famous hierarchy of human needs, the so-called 'Maslow pyramid'. In his pyramid the most basic needs are at the bottom. On top of those are, in order of importance, the other essential needs that need to be fulfilled to be able to live a full life. The highest aim to be achieved in life, according to Maslow, is self-transcendence. This is the need to go beyond yourself by helping others and/or making a connection with something outside yourself, for example in spirituality or religion.

'Levenskunst als grondhouding', managementimpact.nl

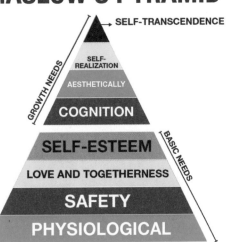

SELF-TRANSCENDENCE
SELF-REALIZATION
AESTHETICALLY
COGNITION
SELF-ESTEEM
LOVE AND TOGETHERNESS
SAFETY
PHYSIOLOGICAL
GROWTH NEEDS
BASIC NEEDS

EVERYTHING UNDER CONTROL?
VERY CORRECT OR SUPER BORING?

Determine at what time you go to bed; don't hang around.	Get up early.	Plan your meals.	Say 'no' sometimes.
Organize your stuff.	Giveaway things you don't need.	Make backups of your photos.	Unsubscribe for notifications.
Read a book.	Automate your payments.	Make to-do lists.	Don't suggest anything.
Make your bed.	Check your mail at set times.	Consume less.	Organize your passwords.
Be grateful.	Make time for the people you love.	Exercise a lot.	Think well.
Don't drink alcohol.	Smile!	Don't compare yourself to others.	Clear up.

> You have become entangled in your own administration of forms to fill out and passwords that give you access to your digital habitat with its hundreds of friends and virtual entertainment. The overload of information, excess intake, crisis, and an overfull agenda have made a mess of your life.
>
> Mieke Gerritzen

CAPITALIST SOCIETY IS SUFFOCATING.
HOW TO PROCEED?

IS YOUR LIFE A MESS?

Tidying up becomes catharsis, cleansing. You're not doing it because it's a mess, but because you want to change your life. Prosperity has brought us full houses and also the Japanese tidying up Guru Marie Kondo. 'In the end, this type of "de-clutterers" remind us of an embarrassing, self-created and stupid luxury problem', says Awee Prins, philosopher and the author of *Uit verveling* (Out of Boredom). 'If we now have to get rid of stuff in a forced manner, it is because we first accumulated all those things like madmen because we thought they would make us happy. But things don't bring happiness.' Man is the malcontent animal, said Dostoyevsky. No matter what situation we find ourselves in, we can always imagine that it could be better. It's what all ideals and utopias are based on and there's nothing wrong with that. It only goes wrong if you start doing this on an ordinary, everyday level: 'When I'm on vacation, I will calm down. If I get rid of my partner, I'll be free. If I change my interior design, my life will become structured.' We always think things will be better if only we change them. Tidying up gurus, de-hasters, and meanwhile we ourselves as well, it seems, always tell us to get rid of something. Of things and of activities. Ignaas Devisch, philosopher and the author of *Rusteloosheid – pleidooi voor een mateloos leven* (Restlessness – A Plea for Boundless Living) describes how our discontent with regard to our own restlessness actually bothers us more than restlessness itself. Perhaps it is this discontent that bothers us much more than our cluttered homes?

Merel Kamp, 'Orde in de ladekast, orde in het leven', *Trouw*

ORGANIZE YOURSELF!

DER MENSCH LEBT DURCH DEN KOPF.

SEIN KOPF REICHT IHM NICHT AUS.

VERSUCH ES NUR, VON DEINEM KOPF

LEBT HÖCHSTENS EINE LAUS.

DENN FÜR DIESES LEBEN

IST DER MENSCH NICHT SCHLAU GENUG.

NIEMALS MERKT ER EBEN

DIESEN LUG UND TRUG.

JA, MACH NUR EINEN PLAN!

SEI NUR EIN GROSSES LICHT!

UND MACH DANN NOCH'NEN ZWEITEN PLAN

GEHN TUN SIE BEIDE NICHT.

DENN FÜR DIESES LEBEN

IST DER MENSCH NICHT SCHLECHT GENUG.

DOCH SEIN HÖHRES STREBEN

IST EIN SCHÖNER ZUG.

JA, RENN NUR NACH DEM GLÜCK

DOCH RENNE NICHT ZU SEHR

DENN ALLE RENNEN NACH DEM GLÜCK

DAS GLÜCK RENNT HINTERHER.

DENN FÜR DIESES LEBEN

IST DER MENSCH NICHT ANSPRUCHSLOS GENUG.

DRUM IST ALL SEIN STREBEN

NUR EIN SELBSTBETRUG.

DER MENSCH IST GAR NICHT GUT

DRUM HAU IHN AUF DEN HUT.

HAST DU IHM AUF DEM HUT GEHAUN

DANN WIRD ER VIELLEICHT GUT.

DENN FÜR DIESES LEBEN

IST DER MENSCH NICHT GUT GENUG

DARUM HAUT IHM EBEN

RUHIG AUF DEN HUT!

Bertolt Brecht, Das Lied von der Unzulänglichkeit des menschlichen Strebens

Make a list of things you plan to do next year. Start with the top one and continue when you've done it. Then strike it off the list.

_____

_____

_____

_____

_____

_____

_____

_____

_____

_____

_____

_____

BETTER LATE THAN NEVER, BUT NEVER LATE IS BETTER.

Warren Buffett

HOW PLAYFUL ARE YOU?

PLAY

ARE YOU A SOCIAL ACTIVIST?

WHAT ROLE DO YOU PLAY?

- CITIZEN
- REFORMER
- REBEL
- CHANGE AGENT

ARE YOU A SOCIAL CREATIVE?

WHAT ROLE DO YOU PLAY?

- CITIZEN
- REFORMER
- REBEL
- CHANGE AGENT

HOW PLAYFUL ARE YOU?

If the word 'play' mainly makes you think of happy screams in a schoolyard or of a group of boys playing a computer game together, then you underestimate how present play is in our daily lives. Play is 'an all-consuming category', according to the Dutch historian Johan Huizinga (1872-1945), who introduced the notion of Homo Ludens. He says that our entire culture in fact consists of play, even originates in play. Although we tend to link play to frivolity, according to Huizinga play is a very serious matter indeed. Play lies at the basis of our everyday actions, from our jobs to parenthood, from sports club to court case.

Source: Elize de Mul, 'Homo Ludens: Je onderschat het belang van spel', Brainwash.nl

HOMO LUDENS
The playful human is a key notion

IS THERE AN ELEMENT OF PLAY IN YOUR WORK?

We can observe elements of play in the most varied cultural forms. In war, for example, or in law. But also in the arts, the economy, in politics or in sports. Think of 'game of politics'. Speaking of which, politicians seem to be increasingly behaving themselves as stars from the entertainment industry, using their 'playful' nature to gain votes. And even when politicians managed to get the content of their message across, the media turned it into a spectacle.

WITH SOME COMPANIES EMPLOYEES HAVE 'UNLIMITED HOLIDAYS', AS MANY DAYS OFF AS THEY LIKE. AND NOT ONLY THAT, THEY HAVE 'BRINGERS OF WORK HAPPINESS' WHO CAN TAKE OVER WHEN EMPLOYEES WANT TO TAKE DAYS OFF. COMPANIES WISH TO CONTRIBUTE TO THE PURPOSE AND WELL-BEING OF THEIR EMPLOYEES.

Ward Janssen

EMPLOYERS BECOME ENJOYERS

DO YOU SPEND MORE TIME ON YOUR SMARTPHONE THAN WITH YOUR FAMILY?

- ☐ YES, BECAUSE ON TWITTER I CHALLENGE PEOPLE.
- ☐ YES, I LIKE TO PARADE MYSELF ON INSTAGRAM.
- ☐ YES, SOCIAL MEDIA ARE MY WINDOW ON SOCIETY.
- ☐ YES, I HAVE NOTHING ELSE TO DO.
- ☐ YES, IT'S MY WORK AS AN INFLUENCER.
- ☐ YES, I DON'T WANT TO MISS ANYTHING.
- ☐ YES, THE FAMILY APP MAKES ME LOOK DIFFERENTLY AT FAMILY.
- ☐ YES, THAT'S RIGHT, BECAUSE MY FAMILY IS AWFUL.

It took me a long time to understand that in so many ways, social media is a game for adults. The hard truth about all this, having hit all the key milestones in my own game, is that it doesn't lead anywhere. It is the emptiest feeling you can imagine. One day you are viral and the next day no one cares again. Much of what you see is fake and it feels wrong. The time commitment to play each version of the game — Facebook, LinkedIn, Twitter, Instagram — is massive. Instead of talking to my family, I'd play social media on my phone. Instead of being creative and doing work that was important to me — such as writing — I'd scroll social media looking for people to follow and things to 'like'. But don't misunderstand me, I'm not saying social media is bad or you should quit it forever. I am also not saying that there are not any benefits. What I'm suggesting is that we need to rethink social media and not play it like it's a computer game for adults. I'm suggesting we change the rules and take social media from being a game to something so much more.

Tim Denning, 'Social Media Is a Computer Game for Adults', medium.com

Image: unknown

Children who are gaming forget their body; they have their screen, their office, and their visual language.

Mieke Gerritzen

DO YOU LOG ON TO THE FRIDAY OFFICE PARTY?

Virtual drinks with friends. Photo: Marcel van den Bergh / de Volkskrant

Via Zoom you join your colleagues on Friday afternoon for a drink, for fun, and against loneliness. Do you sometimes end up drunk at your laptop on your own?

1X☐ 2X☐ 3X☐ 4X☐

DO YOU PLAY WHEN YOU CONSUME?

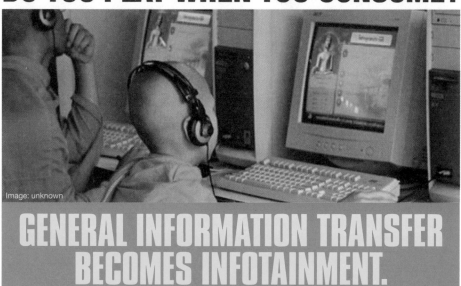

Image: unknown

GENERAL INFORMATION TRANSFER BECOMES INFOTAINMENT.

WHICH DIVERSION IS MORE FUN THAN YOUR SMARTPHONE?

- A MEDITATION SESSION
- BOOZING IT UP
- BUNGEE JUMPING
- HOLDING A PROTEST MARCH
- JUICE FASTING IN TURKEY
- CONVERTING TO RELIGION
- GARDENING
- KNITTING CAFÉ

playworks.org

deepplayforkids.com

PLAY IS A FORM OF VALUE, AND VALUE BEGETS DIGNITY AND NEEDS VIRTUE.

Tom Apperley in Victor-Navarro Remesal, 'A Philosophy of Play', medium.com

DOES YOUR WORLD IMPROVE WITH *PLAY?*

Huizinga saw the advent of technology as one of the major threats to play. At the same time, we see how the Internet is actually 'ludifying' society. Everything has to be fun. While plodding along and building a career we send each other cat gifs to break the day's monotony. Selfies on Instagram, silly Facebook news items — are these the characteristics of a reviving, playful mankind or are they symptoms of an age of a childish mankind? Or are they office jokes in a competitive world?

'De spelende mens, documentaire en gesprek met Elize de Mul en Léon Hanssen', lux-nijmegen.nl

IS EVERYTHING REALLY MORE FUN?

Gamification is the application of game-design elements and game principles in non-game contexts (such as navigation apps, social media, and in scientific studies) in order to influence human behaviour in a positive manner.

Wikipedia.org

FUN IS COMPULSORY!

ARE YOU REALLY GOING TO LIKE THINGS THAT ARE NOT FUNNY AT ALL?

INSPIRE YOURSELF!
PLACE THE FOLLOWING NON-FUN THINGS IN AN ORDER YOU LIKE.
IT'S A FUN THING TO DO!

1.	cooking if you have to	1. ....
2.	sitting out a long zoom session	2. ....
3.	organizing your birthday	3. ....
4.	doing things if you don't feel like it	4. ....
5.	clearing up & cleaning	5. ....
6.	doing paperwork	6. ....
7.	arriving on time	7. ....
8.	being nice under stress	8. ....
9.	getting up	9. ....
10.	returning items to IKEA	10. ....
11.	going to a 5-hour dinner	11. ....
12.	clearing out the dishwasher	12. ....
13.	looking at bad art	13. ....
14.	holding onto a bullshit job	14. ....

The playful man is a classic utopian image in which man embraces his frivolity, freed from his working life full of performance, social pressure, social conventions, and self-discipline.

Ward Janssen

POWER, PRIME MINISTERS AND THE PRESS
ROBERT LEWIS
The Battle for Truth on Parliament Hill
Stokely Carmichael & Charles V. Hamilton
Black Power
The Politics of Liberation in America
THE POWER OF NOW
CLAIM YOUR POWER
MASTIN KIPP'S
THE POWER OF YOUR SUB CONSCIOUS MIND
HITLER AND STALIN
ALAN BULLOCK
LOVE, SEX, MONEY, and POWER
EDWARD B. ALLEN
ANTHONY ROBBINS
DEEPAK CHOPRA
Self POWER
Spiritual solutions to life's greatest challenges
POWER PLAYBOOK
THE POWER OF PASSIVE INCOME
MAKE YOUR MONEY WORK FOR YOU
Nightingale-Conant
HOW TO CHOOSE A LEADER
Maurizio Viroli
POWER
LENDING POWER
Money, Power and Sex

DO YOU HAVE HAVE POWER OVER YOURSELF?

POWER

For years I dreamed of having power
Power to create what I want to see myself
That makes it part of me, it becomes my own
Then I will get the honour or derision I deserve

Power to control every detail
Every element of the whole package
To be able to turn the tide in adversary
Quality control from A to Z

I want power, I know what is best
I want power, I proposed that from now on I will decide for
everyone else

Power all too often leads to arrogance
But I'm too smart for that, it won't happen to me
I am a great champion of tolerance, you see
Although I have the biggest mouth

I want power, which I will use for the good
I want power, everything under my control
I want power, this hurt I aim to keep
I want power (but it's addictive, I keep wanting more)

My world will be a lot better than, thanks to me
My world will be a lot more complete, thanks to me

I make the new laws, I make the world go round
No one will stand in my way, I know which way the wind
blows

I want power, which I will use for the good
I want power, everything under my control
I want power, this hurt I aim to keep
I want power (but it's addictive, I keep wanting more)
I want power (but it's addictive, I keep wanting more)
I want power (but it's addictive, I keep wanting more)

Karin Bloemen, *Ik wil macht,* muzikum.eu

WHAT DO YOU WANT?

○ **AUTONOMY**

○ **INFLUENCE**

WHAT DO YOU HAVE?

○ **MONEY**

○ **ARROGANCE**

○ **FAME**

○ **DISCIPLINE**

○ **KNOWLEDGE**

○ **GUTS**

○ **OVERVIEW**

○ **VISION**

WOULD YOU LIKE TO BE MORE IMPORTANT THAN YOU REALLY ARE?

☐ YES ☐ NO

MOTIVATE _____

ARE YOU OVERBLOWN?

Being too big for your boots is a form of arrogance, wanting to look bigger and more important than you actually are. The feeling that you are important is mostly imaginary. But for whom? Who benefits from it? An overblown self-image that does not coincide with a real self. A balloon, a bit of hot air. In *Die Stadt hinter dem Strom* (The City Behind the Stream) (1947) the German author Herman Kasack describes a life after death and all the Nazis are floating around there like blown-up balloons. They don't actually exist anymore, they have become air, hot air. But in addition to the enlargement of the self in your own head, the self-image that spreads and takes on huge proportions, of a usurper, a world conqueror—and what is conquering but a concrete as well as fictional enlargement of the self— there is also a religiously motivated blowing up of the self. Every ideology, every faith, every religion, every trust in higher powers and every confirmation of being part of a greater whole is in fact a form of blowing up of the self. Your own body limits are no longer the last and final frontier of the self. All of a sudden, the self is part of a larger self, a self that considerably transcends the individual self. This may provide pleasant feelings, security, you name it, but also unpleasant ones, unease, feeling imprisoned within, and so on. Self and self-image, self-image and worldview are closely related here. It colours and/or darkens your life: both, as this may all turn out either positive or negative. It is an attempt to go beyond the limitations of the self that is bound to the physical body and to finiteness, with varying results. Is that smart? I don't know. You will find out soon enough when making up the balance of your life, at least if you haven't chosen a different, radical solution before then, such as the self-blow-up-terrorist.

John Hacking, 'Het opgeblazen zelf', levenshorizonten.com

DO YOU WANT POWER?

☐ YES, BECAUSE I FEEL SUPERIOR
☐ YES, BECAUSE I AM VERY INTELLIGENT
☐ YES, BECAUSE I SEE WHAT OTHERS DON'T SEE
☐ YES, BECAUSE PEOPLE LOOK UP TO ME
☐ YES, BECAUSE RULING IS MY NATURE

WHO ARE YOU?

☐ THE POLITICIAN

Driven by influence and a theatrical energy; a newsworthy opinion leader who can be a hardliner or chooses the compromise of the backroom.

☐ THE DICTATOR

An out-of-control politician and coup stager who rules by fear, supported by an army of insiders and the military.

☐ THE TYCOON

Operating far above or at state level, with large capital and major interests. Relentlessly working for stockholders and profit margins.

☐ THE CELEBRITY

Powerful by adoration, somtimes as a spokesperson or political supporter, highly influential, even if only from an indirect position of power.

☐ THE MANAGER

Process inhibiting, proud figure. Knows nothing of contents, but knows his tools and make sure that the organization's policy is implemented.

☐ THE BUREAUCRAT

An unscrupulous person, imposing and implementing rules, for whom orders are orders. Maintains a radical distinction between his work and his private life.

☐ THE SURGEON

Clinically and emotionally isolated in order to achieve perfection. Emphatic and only by appointment.

DO YOU PLAY THE POWER GAME?

ARE YOU THE GENIUS ACTOR WHO IMITATES A POWER FIGURE IN THE CURRENT MEDIA AGE?

YOU ARE A SELF-FACILITATING *MEDIA NODE*

Nathan Barley

DO MEN NEED POWER MORE THAN WOMEN?

Transgender men claim that a testosterone treatment definitely has a certain effect. Maxim Februari (formerly a woman) experienced how you suddenly are brimming with an irrationally high self-confidence, think you are the centre of the world and that everyone will love you, and how everything excites you.

The Frenchman Michel Foucault (1926–1984) is one of the most influential philosophers of our age. He showed how power plays a role in all human relationships. In the 1970s this was a ground-breaking insight, as the general feeling was that we were all equal. Foucault showed that institutions discipline us. This is evident from the #MeToo discussion. In the 1960s it was not uncommon for a therapist to sleep with a patient, or for a teacher to sleep with a student. We were all equal, right? Thanks to Foucault we now understand that such relationships are not equal.

Source: Leonie Breebaart, 'Wat Michel Foucault niet zag: macht uitoefenen is niet hetzelfde als geweld gebruiken', *Trouw*

HAVE YOU EVER HAD SEX WITH SOMEONE WHO AT THE TIME HAD A LOWER POSITION THAN YOU?

☐ YES ☐ NO

MOTIVATE _____

HOW POWERFUL IS TECHNOLOGY?

'Technology flourishes in times of crisis. So do its negative sides: people fear the news, are digitally vulnerable, hackers are active, there's a lot of phishing going on, hospitals are digitally attacked, it's all happening. The best and the worst of technology are now converging.' In Taiwan you get a visit from the police when your phone's battery is empty. We have to be careful in Europe not to copy such authoritarian practices. If you are aware that phone data are valuable, you have to design a proper framework for using that information. However, there is a tendency to do it the other way around: go ahead, we'll see whether it is useful afterwards. But once such power is granted, it is rarely ever withdrawn.'

Marietje Schaake in Huib Modderkolk, 'Privacy-expert Marietje Schaake: "Bedrijven en overheden zijn altijd op zoek naar meer online macht"', *de Volkskrant*

YOUR SMARTPHONE KNOWS:

WHAT YOU BUY
HOW MUCH MONEY YOU HAVE
WHAT YOU EAT
HOW MUCH YOU WEIGH
WHO YOU KNOW
WHERE YOU ARE
WHAT YOU SEE
WHAT AIR YOU BREATHE
WHEN YOU EXERCISE
YOUR CALORIE INTAKE
WITH WHOM YOU ARGUE
WHETHER YOU'RE PREGNANT
WHAT YOUR DESIRES ARE
WHAT YOU THINK

DO YOU HAVE POWER OVER YOURSELF?

● **YES** ● **NO**

IS SUCCESS YOUR GOAL?

SUCCESS

DEEP DOWN YOU KNOW THAT YOU CAN'T FORCE SUCCESS. SUCCESS IS AN EXTRA, A CONSEQUENCE.

ARE YOU SECRETELY WORKING ON SUCCESS?

 YES, I WANT FAME AND WEALTH.

MOTIVATE _____

 NO, NOT AT ALL!

MOTIVATE _____

IN THE ACHIEVEMENT-ORIENTED SOCIETY YOU NEED TO SCORE.

 YES, I HAVE TO REACH THE TARGETS SET BY THE MARKETING DEPARTMENT

MOTIVATE _____

 NO, I SET MY OWN GOALS IN TERMS OF CONTENT.

MOTIVATE _____

SUCCESS AS IT IS BEING PRESCRIBED IS A MARKETING VEHICLE

ARE YOU CARRIED AWAY BY AN OVERHEATED PERFORMANCE SOCIETY?

SET YOUR GOALS!

SUCCESS IS A CONSEQUENCE.

That the earth is not the centre of the universe has been known for centuries. But that mankind is not the crown of creation — that is a conclusion we are still struggling with, although Charles Darwin already said so. Post humanists show us a different way of looking at the world when we no longer see ourselves as its centre. That you are not the centre of the world and that mankind is not what the universe is all about, puts everything that goes on in your head is perspective, literally and figuratively. This, for when you are once more about to get carried away by the prevailing urge to perform in our society. Success is a consequence, never the goal.

Source: Ernst-Jan Pfauth, 'Prestatiemaatschappij', decorrespondent.nl

WHAT IS YOUR GOAL?

- ○ I WANT SUCCESS, BECAUSE I'M PRETTY.
- ○ I WANT SUCCESS, BECAUSE I'M A GENIUS.
- ○ I WANT SUCCESS, BECAUSE I DO GOOD.
- ○ I WANT SUCCESS, BECAUSE I MAKE A LOT OF MONEY.
- ○ I WANT SUCCESS, BECAUSE I AM A WINNER.
- ○ I WANT SUCCESS, BECAUSE I'M GOING TO BE FAMOUS.
- ○ I WANT SUCCESS FOR THE SAKE OF SUCCESS.

The road to only success is an illusion and is a self-help method that encourages you to buy one self-help book about success after the other.

Mieke Gerritzen

LOTS OF SUCCESS!

EXIT
STRATEGY

We are all struggling with our search for success. Perhaps you will be replaced by technology, so you had better work out an EXIT STRATEGY for yourself. It is far from easy to step out successfully and timely when the world changes. In the start-up culture you do not strive to build a beautiful company that you will be running with great joy until you die; no, you try to achieve the exact growth curve that makes your company worth buying: your exit is a deal worth millions and then you can take a step back, or retire. This growth curve is called the HYPE CYCLE and its every venture capitalist's wet dream. Silicon Valley's success formula is first and foremost an arms race by investors to be their first and get out with the loot at the right time. AFTER YOU THE DELUGE. Ward Janssen

DETOX YOUR EGO!

DEALING WITH THE PUMP & DUMP EGO BESTSELLER

Geert Lovink

DO YOU CONSUME LITTLE BITS OF SUCCESS VIA SOCIAL

YES, BECAUSE I GET MANY LIKES.

MOTIVATE _____

NO, NOT AT ALL!

MOTIVATE *SUCCES OP SOCIAL MEDIA IS TOCH FLAUWEKUL?*

WHY WE SHOULD STOP CELEBRATING CONSUMERISM

Joshua Becker, ' Why We Should Stop Celebrating Consumentism', forbes.com

MORENEWBETTER!

After World War II, consumer spending no longer meant just satisfying an indulgent material desire. In fact, the American consumer was praised as a patriotic citizen in the 1950s, contributing to the ultimate success of the American way of life. 'The good purchaser devoted to "more, newer and better" was the good citizen', historian Lizabeth Cohen explained, 'since economic recovery after a decade and a half of depression and war depended on a dynamic mass consumption economy.'

'The Rise of American Consumerism', pbs.org

YOU ARE NOT A PRODUCT OF YOUR CIRCUMSTANCES. YOU ARE A PRODUCT OF YOUR DECISIONS.

Source: Stephen R. Covey, 'An Effective Life'

SUCCESSFUL PEOPLE   UNSUCCESSFUL PEOPLE

SUCCESSFUL PEOPLE	UNSUCCESSFUL PEOPLE
Read every day	Watch TV every day
Compliment	Criticize
Embrace Change	Fear change
Forgive others	Hold a grudge
Talk about ideas	Talk about people
Continuously learn	Think they know it all
Accept responsibility for their failures	Blame others for their failures
Have a sense of gratitude	Have a sense of entitlement
Set goals and develop life plans	Never set goals

John Paul DeJoria, '9 Key Differences Between Successful And Unsuccessful People', healthyfoodhouse.com

Einstein said that 'Imagination is more important than knowledge'. The more vividly and accurately you imagine your success, the easier it will be for the rest of yourself to follow through.

TRY   FAIL   TRY AGAIN   SUCCESS

WHAT IS SUCCESS FOR YOU?

Are you overly sensitive to success and to failure?

I OFTEN HAVE TO CRY WHEN I'M SUCCESSFUL.

○ strongly agree ○ agree ○ somewhat agree or disagree ○ disagree ○ strongly disagree

I FEEL HUMILIATED WHEN CRITICIZED.

○ strongly agree ○ agree ○ somewhat agree or disagree ○ disagree ○ strongly disagree

I AM JALOUS OF SUCCESSFUL PEOPLE.

○ strongly agree ○ agree ○ somewhat agree or disagree ○ disagree ○ strongly disagree

I AM ASHAMED OF FAILURE, BUT NOBODY NOTICES.

○ strongly agree ○ agree ○ somewhat agree or disagree ○ disagree ○ strongly disagree

I BEGRUDGE OTHER PEOPLE THEIR SUCCESS.

○ strongly agree ○ agree ○ somewhat agree or disagree ○ disagree ○ strongly disagree

I DON'T LIKE SHARING MY SUCCESS WITH OTHERS.

○ strongly agree ○ agree ○ somewhat agree or disagree ○ disagree ○ strongly disagree

I TRY TO AVOID FAILURE, NO MATTER WHAT.

○ strongly agree ○ agree ○ somewhat agree or disagree ○ disagree ○ strongly disagree

QUESTIONS FROM THE 'HOW NARCICISTIC AM I?' TEST

ARE YOU A JUNKIE?

ADDICTION

ARE YOU A SLAVE OR ADDICTED?

You may reach a phase in your life when it seems as if you are fenced in and limited. You feel like you can't go on, mentally. ... You may be challenged by tests that may seem enormous and limit you to such a degree that you can't make a breakthrough and find a solution for your problems. Freedom or slavery are issues that you meet in your daily life, as it were. Especially in your generation, when everything is possible, you can easily become a slave to society or, worse, to your own inclinations.

In order to understand how someone can be a slave to his own inclinations, you should think of the distinction between a human being and an animal. An animal does have a mind, but that mind is overruled by its instinct. When it needs food, its brain makes sure that it knows where to find it and how to take it. If it needs protection it knows how to defend itself and, if necessary, where to find shelter. If it wants attention, it will learn how and where, et cetera, et cetera. With an animal, the mind only works as a means to obtain its emotional or material needs.

Humans are not four-footed animals. With humans the brain is higher up than the heart. Humans must be higher than animals. In the human body the head is, both literally and figuratively speaking, above the heart.

Likewise, the human mind should be superior to material lusts. If people use their minds only to execute their instincts and emotions, they degrade themselves lower than the animals. After all, animals are created in such a way that their intellect is dominated by emotions. Animals do not have the possibility of acting otherwise. A human being who lets his emotions dominate his intellect is worse than an animal because as a human being he has the possibility of acting otherwise, namely to ensure that his intellect has the upper hand. Still, you often see someone seeing what they want and then use their mind to reason and to rationalize that the thing they wants is also right. The eye sees; the heart desires and the hand takes. He has made the human within himself a slave to his material and emotional needs. He is no different from a developed animal. Like the animal, whose instincts tells it that it needs food and then uses its mind to heed his needs, humans use their intellect to realize their lusts. They make themselves slaves to their instincts and emotions. They do what feels good, no matter the consequences and in some cases they ruin their whole life and happiness. Chain-smoking or even drugs, crime and other mental and emotional problems can also be the result sometimes of 'doing what you feel like at that moment'.

You think you are free then, but in fact the opposite is true: someone who always acts upon what his heart tells him will slowly but surely become a slave to his own emotions. He gets so used to doing what he feels like that whenever he wants to act differently, he can't summon the energy to keep his desires under control. Some people are victim to a different kind of slavery: they don't really have an opinion of their own. There 'opinion' mainly consists of mimicking what they hear around them, in which radio, TV and newspapers often play a major part. These people are not really free either; unfortunately, they are not even aware of their own opinion. If someone wants to be free of his 'addiction' it does not suffice to suppress material and/or emotional lusts. They must also try to find a positive goal in their lives.

Source: Rabbi A.L. Heintz, 'Slavernij en verslaving', joodsleven.nl

Your blue check marks haunt me in my sleepless nights.

Swiping fingers assist to move the mind elsewhere. Checking the smartphone is the present way of daydreaming.

Geert Lovink, *Sad by Design*

DOES ENDLESS SCROLLING FEEL LIKE DRUGS?

☐ **YES** ☐ **NO**

MOTIVATE _____

It's as if they're pouring cocaine all over your interface.

Tech companies want to make people addicted. This goes so deep that they even tinker with the colour and shape of the Like button. Former president Sean Parker has described Facebook strategy as 'exploiting a weak spot in the human psyche'. Both employers and founders are aware of this, 'and yet we kept doing it'.

Source: Isobel Asher Hamilton, 'Facebook, Snapchat en Twitter zetten bewust verslavende technieken in om van gebruikers 'sociale junkies' te maken', businessinsider.nl

IN CONSUMING INFORMATION, HABIT AND ADDICTION ARE MIXED.

EVERYONE IS ADDICTED!

A modern addiction seems to be quite different from a traditional addiction. You don't need to be traumatized to get a kick out of gaming or staring at your smartphone. And if you're hooked on Facebook you are not necessarily suppressing nasty feelings. Binge watching series is not necessarily the result of feeling bad. Modern addictive behaviour is mainly governed by reward: the dopamine effect. It's not about some substance that is addictive, such as alcohol, tobacco, or other drugs, but about your own behaviour that becomes addictive. This behaviour has the same rewarding effect as taking a shot and behaviour is an activity that is overvalued by the brain. This behaviour does the same thing the needle did that stimulated the reward centre nucleus accumbens with addicted mice in 1954: nothing mattered anymore; they didn't eat, didn't sleep, everything was about having that nice feeling. They died from exhaustion. Likewise, lengthy gaming can cause death by a blood clot that is released. Another difference is that a traditional addiction is usually seen as morally reprehensible. You should quit it completely. Not so in modern addictions. Gaming, shopping, wrapping — all great fun!

Carien Karsten, 'Hoe moet je omgaan met moderne verslavingen?', intermediair.nl

Is the massive addiction to information really an addiction? ● YES ● NO
Or should we start thinking differently about addiction? ● YES ● NO

WE LIVE IN A TIME OF EMOTIONAL CAPITALISM.

'Our brains are prediction machines. When we receive a reward, the first time we get it, they want us to do it again. Over time, with repetition, we go to anticipating that reward as opposed to actually getting it.'

Dr. Judson Brewer in Kate Green Trip, 'Untangling Love Addiction in the Brain', medium.com

HOW NUMB ARE YOU?

Our entire western society is in the grip of the addiction to money, material things, and consumption, and of the 'principle of economic growth' that is supposed to maintain this addiction. The consequences in many areas are horrendous; we can really call them black, but we choose to collectively ignore this. We see people who are addicted to work, to their family, to status, to erudition, to poverty, to top achievements in sports, to idiotic and extreme feats just to be in the *Guinness Book of Records*, to… You can name just about everything, because anything can be used as an anaesthetic.

Koert van Mensvoort

OUR ECONOMIES ARE FINANCIALLY, POLITICALLY AND SOCIALLY ADDICTED TO ENDLESS GROWTH.

Babies start by crawling, become stronger, and then they pull themselves up and stand. And we applaud them. Moving forward and then up is the most important form of progress in the human body. And we tell the same story about ourselves as a species. From our bent-over ancestors up to Homo erectus, who stood upright. Then came we, Homo sapiens — always on the way to the future. It's also in our language: 'Why are you so down? Did you have to take a step back? Chin up. We are making progress again.' It's no wonder that we always strive for progress and that we also represent the success of our economy as a forward motion, a rising line.

Source: Kate Raworth, 'Waarom de economie niet alleen om groei draait', brainwash.nl

SOCIETY, THAT'S YOU. STOP GROWTH! ENOUGH IS ENOUGH!

WHAT ARE YOU ADDICTED TO?

ALCOHOL	FITNESS
GAMING	SMARTPHONE
NEWS	FAMILY
FACEBOOK	EXPENSIVE THINGS
SUN HOLIDAYS	NEW CLOTHES
RUNNING	GRAY SHRIMPS
LIQUORICE	BIOPRODUCTS
CANNABIS	SHOPPING
NAILBITING	SALTED CARAMEL
DRUGS	ORDERING ONLINE
FLYING	BEETHOVEN
NETFLIX	JEWELLERY
BUYING	ROSÉ
SEX	OPENINGS
EATING	ZOOM MEETINGS
CHOCOLATE	SUBSIDY
CARS	PANCAKES
SLEEPING	SNEAKERS
SKIING	MAGAZINES
SELF-HELP BOOKS	PHILOSOPHY
SMOKING	DEVICES
FLOSSING	CHEESE
CLEARING UP	RITUALS
CAT VIDEOS	PRIMARK
WORK	CREAM
SWIMMING	COFFEE
MERGERS	RESTAURANTS

IS YOUR DEPRESSION AN OPPOR- TUNITY?

DEPRESSION

KwangHo Shin, *Untitled*, 2013

#NOFILTER

CAN YOU RECOGNIZE DEPRESSION?

I'm Not Mad.

Or Am I?

Andrew Salomon, *The Noonday Demon*

DEPRESSION IS MELANCHOLY MINUS ITS CHARMS.

Susan Sontag, *Illness as Metaphor*

ARE YOU EVER DEPRESSED?
◯ Yes ◯ No ◯ ??

'I NEVER ACTUALLY FELT I WAS SOMEONE TO HAVE A DEPRESSION. I NEVER SAW MYSELF LIKE THAT.'

Joost Zwagerman in Tom Kellerhuis, 'Zelfmoord beschouw ik als no-go-area', *HP/De Tijd*

Are you frequently down?

Are you the millennial with choice stress?

Are you the doubting allrounder?

WILL YOUR SMARTPHONE PREDICT THE ONSET OF A DEPRESSION?

☐ YES ☐ NO

MOTIVATE

'So much is recorded about psychiatric patients that by using smart data analyses and text mining you can use that information for the benefit of the treatment.' 'This could lead, for example, to a different approach in preventing aggression. When we link this information to other data sources, such as the weather, air quality, demographic data, and figures on the economic situation, we become increasingly better at recognizing patterns in patients.' 'But we cannot predict when and if someone will have a depression.' 'Many disorders seem to have sudden transitions. It's like coming closer and closer to the abyss. If you take one step too many, you're gone. The fact that you are coming closer and closer to that abyss can be visualized through self-monitoring. This implies that you receive a warning when things start to go wrong. How to visualize and use that warning for the patient is something we still need to learn.'

Floor Scheepers and Peter Groot in Frederieke Jacobs, 'Weet je smartphone of je depressief bent?', smarthealth.nl

WHERE ARE YOU WHEN YOU ARE DEPRESSED:

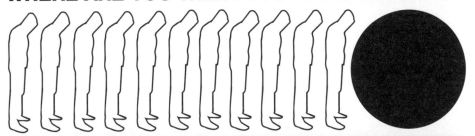

BLACK BILE

Having a lot of black bile of good temperature, Aristotle thought, enabled a person to perform great feats and achieve great wisdom. But if black bile became either too hot or too cold, it was a dangerous, pathogenic substance. Much black bile gives inspiration, the words start to flow, the metaphors become richer, the imagination is unleashed. One reaches a state of creative exaltation that can lead to poetic ecstasy. The link between black bile and special intellectual and creative achievements is a fiction of Aristotle's imagination.

Andy Lameijn, 'Zwarte gal en glazen billen', biomaatschappij.n

DOES GLOOM MAKE YOU EXTRA CREATIVE?

'We know that people who suffer from depression often feel that they are not under-stood, that they feel cut off from the world, unable to make contact anymore. Those who suffer from depression, are sometimes compelled to focus on themselves. In his study "Experiences of Depression" the philosopher Matthew Ratcliffe writes about the social paradox of depression: feeling a connection is the hardest thing while at the same time it often is the patients' deepest wish. Everyday language is often not sufficient for patients to correctly imprecisely express their feelings. Literature provides patients with not only a companion in misery but also with a new, pre-formed language for their suffering. Thanks to literature depression as the chaotic, the meaningless, is being related to the opposite notions of the stylized, the artistic, the beautiful and meaningful.'

Reading autobiographies can help against depression. Peter Henk Steenhuis26 november 2018 Trouw.nl

I am unable to describe exactly what is the matter with me. Now and then there are horrible fits of anxiety, apparently without cause.

Vincent van Gogh

The painting is thought to represent the angst of modern man, which Munch experienced deeply throughout his life, but saw as an indispensable driver of his art. He wrote in his diary:

'My fear of life is necessary to me, as is my illness. They are indistinguishable from me, and their destruction would destroy my art.'

Edvard Munch

William Lee Adams, 'The Dark Side of Creativity', cnn.com

The sun began to set — suddenly the sky turned blood red. I stood there trembling with anxiety and I sensed an endless scream passing through nature.

Edvard Munch in his diary, 22 January 1892

EVERY DEPRESSION HAS A RHYTHM, AND IT'S DIFFERENT FOR EVERYONE.

Try and find your rhythm by naming the phases in order.

searching
adapting
falling
getting up
relapsing
accepting
letting go
fighting
waiting
finding yourself again
making mistakes
allowing
setting goals
persevering
reconciling
sleeping
asking questions
crying
committing
finding strength
not giving up
being active
loving
feeling worry free
putting up with misery
isolating
avoiding
finding out
thinking
feeling nothing
having attention
tasting
coming back
ignoring
leaving
being
doing
awakening

_____
_____
_____
_____
_____
_____
_____
_____
_____
_____
_____
_____
_____
_____
_____
_____
_____

**Depression is a dark tunnel where the light at the end is hard to find.
But it's not impossible. It can be defeated.
Because you are stronger than the illness.**

ARE YOU AFRAID OF YOURSELF?

FEAR

ARE YOU AFRAID OF:

please check

☐ TERRORISM
☐ THE CLIMATE
☐ MICROBES
☐ PROPERTY
☐ THE POLICE
☐ FLIES
☐ SPIDERS
☐ POVERTY
☐ ADDICTION
☐ COVID-19
☐ NATIONALISM
☐ THOUGHTS
☐ PROSPERITY

THERE HAS ALWAYS BEEN FEAR

FEAR OF COMMUNISM
DE ATOM BOMB DE RUSSIANS
THE CHINESE SEXUALITY
DEATH CHANGE
YOUNG PEOPLE CANCER
FEAR FOR NOTHING

Harry Mulisch, *De toekomst van gisteren*

DO YOU CONTROL YOUR FEARS?

○ YES, REGULATION IS A SOLUTION TO ALL MY FEARS.

○ YES, I BUY OFF MY INSECURITIES WITH CHEAP INSURANCE POLICIES.

○ YES, I CONTROL MY FEARS AND IN EXCHANGE I GIVE UP MY FREEDOMS.

FEAR IS A PRODUCT
ALL RISK!

Security and insurance companies are profiting from it. No other people in the world spend as much on insurance policies as the Dutch. Preferably, we would not only like to be insured against real dangers but also against imaginative ones.

Ewoud Butter, 'Angst verkoopt', republiekallochtonie.nl

THE ONLY THING WE HAVE TO FEAR IS FEAR ITSELF.
Franklin D. Roosevelt in his first inaugural address, 1933

EVERY DAY, DO SOMETHING YOU ARE AFRAID OF.
Eleanor Roosevelt

FEAR FOR FUN

It is the dark side of social reality that makes horror so appealing to us. Everyone knows subconsciously that modernity, with its ideals of makeability, order, and transparency is just an island in a sea of dark forces, of decay, anarchy, and uncontrollability.

P.H. Lovecraft

Geert Wilders as the Joker

Creepy Evil Granny: Scary Horror Game

Chucky

Kim Myatt

FEAR IS CONTAGIOUS

Gruesome entertainment is an aesthetic experience, which, according to the German philosopher Immanuel Kant is related to the belief that our reason is superior to nature. We can experience this feeling, for example when we are at the edge of a cliff or on a bridge high above a fast-flowing river. If we would fall down, we would be irrevocably lost. Our physical powerlessness vis-a-vis nature creates a horror. But at the same time the idea that we can decide ourselves whether to jump or not is strangely attractive. We can decide ourselves whether we will let ourselves be destroyed and in that sense we are superior to nature. The feeling of the sublime is the quick alternation of repulsion and pleasure.

Luuk Koelman, 'Niets is zo besmettelijk als angst', universonline.nl

AVOID HYSTERICAL NEWS REPORTS!

Fear of the future, of pain and being mortal are real forces in society and facts alone can't save us.

Nynke van Verschuer, 'Hoe angst de wereld veroverde', *NRC Handelsblad*

AFRAID OF THE NEWS?

WHO OR WHAT SCARES YOU?

☐ **POWER FIGURES**
☐ **RACISM**
☐ **DISASTERS**
☐ **CLIMATE CHANGE**
☐ **SYSTEMS**
☐ **ROBOTS**

Lars Duursma and Job ten Bosch, 'Ook jij kunt angst zaaien en invloed oogsten', *NRC Handelsblad*

We are infecting one another with fear and anxiety, which is spreading faster than a virus.

Andy Martin, 'Coronavirus. The First Post-Truth Pandemic Tinged with Brexit Thinking', *Independent*

SCARED TO DEATH OF FAILURE?

stop striving!

CONTROL, INSECURITY, FEAR OF FAILURE, AND PERFECTIONISM WILL END IN STRESS

PHOBOPHOBIA

Do you respond with fear to the world because of the pressure that is put on you to survive and to succeed? Are you perhaps afraid of not being accepted in society? Phobophobia is the fear of fear itself. Panophobia is the fear of everything that might happen. The philosopher Kierkegaard talked about the state of being as 'the vertigo of freedom' and called fear itself 'an unrest that lives within myself'. Source: 'Phobophobia', nl.qwe.wiki

My right to defend myself and my body supersedes your ignorance and fear of guns.

PRODUCTS OF FEAR

The fearful world during the COVID-19 crisis:
Europeans are stockpiling toilet paper and frozen peas.
Americans are stockpiling guns and revolvers.

FEAR IS UNHAPPINESS. THAT IS WHY NOT COURAGE BUT THE ABSENCE OF FEAR IS HAPPINESS.

Franz Kafka in his diary, 18 January 1922

CHOOSE AN EVENT:

1. COVID-19 PANDEMIC
2. A MURDER IN YOUR FAMILY
3. 9/11 NEW YORK 2001
4. FINANCIAL PROBLEM

FOLLOW THE SCHEME:

Event Where was I, with whom, what happened?	
Thoughts What went through my head? What did I think? How did I feel about it?	
Feelings What did I feel? Which emotions did I have?	
Behaviour What did I do? How did I react?	
Result What was the result of what I did or how I reacted?	

DO YOU REALLY EXIST?

TRUTH

The Earth is flat.

Robots take over your job.

Fiction is the new reality.

All information is propaganda.

Trump was elected by a majority.

God exists.

Fake meat tastes good.

The Holocaust was a Jewish conspiracy.

Bread is bad for you.

Cultivated meat stimulates cannibalism.

The first human to reach 150 is already born.

Alcohol is just as bad as cigarettes.

9/11 was a hoax.

Nationalism is well-intended.

Digitalization reduces humans to empty husks.

Text is disappearing.

The earth is warming up.

70 is the new 50.

COVID-19 is over.

Soon we'll be travelling to Mars.

ARE YOU A *'TRUTHER'*?

☐ **YES**   ☐ **NO**

MOTIVATE

We are raised by the world of commercials and we know that every fine promise, either in HD or traditional Technicolor, is just pulling our leg. But does this also apply to science? And is therefore all information propaganda? 'Truthers' often are especially deniers of major events in recent history. 9/11 was a hoax. The Holocaust a Jewish conspiracy. Denying the Holocaust is punishable by law but the Internet makes the truther movements flexible and evasive. Spreading fake arguments via huge open platforms and numerous blogs has become so easy that it looks like it can't be stopped. Even the Flat Earth movement is growing. The algorithms used by YouTube automatically point to similar videos that keep confirming these conspiracy theories.

Source: Jonathan Kay, *Among the Truthers*

SINCE I KNOW THAT NO ONE IS INTERESTED IN THE TRUTH, I DON'T LIE ANYMORE.

Koos van Zomeren, *Een jaar in scherven*

FICTION IS ALSO TRUE.

'For me fiction represents power, the power of language. What you see on social media now, that's all language, and it has intentions. The intention to hurt, to review, to revile, to be cynical. All that belongs to the domain of fiction, in my view. Gossip is also fiction, but gossip can destroy lives.'

Connie Palmen in Wilma de Rek, 'Roem, een belangrijk thema in het werk van Connie Palmen', *de Volkskrant*

As long as you believe in Santa you will get presents.

Sietse Visser

DO YOU SEEK THE TRUTH?

You look at the world from your personal perspective. You live in your own truth, as it were, and you can distort this truth. This may sound strange but you can make yourself believe truths simply through repetition and conviction. Think of yourself as a bouncy ball that is being influenced by all sorts of things. You bump against walls, roll down the hill, or get stuck in the mud. You will arrive at the truth when you begin to realize, slowly but surely, what obstacles are influencing you and in which direction they point. You think that you are already aware of things, but you should first find out if this is truly the case.

'Wat is waarheid?', naturerunswild.com

DO YOU FREQUENTLY BLUFF?

- Out of self-confidence.
- You often pretend.
- Out of insecurity.
- When you do something new.
- Quite unconsciously.
- When you want to learn something.
- Sometimes you feel like Superman.
- After a testosterone shot.
- If you try to be more than you are.

DO YOU LIE TO YOURSELF?

THE TRUTH LIES IN THE MIDDLE, SURROUNDED BY OTHER LIES.

Karel Jonckheere

DO THOSE IN POWER DECIDE WHAT IS TRUE?

The truth is not fixed, it is 'malleable' and subject to change. Michel Foucault (French philosopher) says that determining the truth is in many cases related to power. Power is being able to determine what is true and then embed it in society. People who create and determine the truth can do so because they are in social positions that give them this power.

Frans Wulffele, 'Michel Foucault: macht bepaalt wat kennis is', franswulffele.nl

DEEP FAKES

DON'T BELIEVE EVERYTHING!

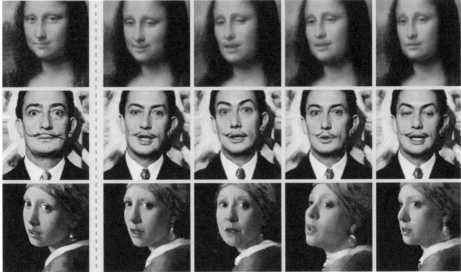

Deepfakes generated from a single image (left) by Egor Zakharov, Aliaksandra Shysheya, and Egor Burkov

'Deep fake' is the umbrella term for software that allows you to make fake videos that are practically indistinguishable from real. With this software you can have someone say or do things that he or she has never said or done in reality. Before, you would only find this type of software in expensive Hollywood film studios, but nowadays it can be downloaded for free and used by anyone. Deep fakes, and fake news, can convince people of things that never took place or that no one ever said. At worst it would mean that everything may be fake. The media, politics, and democracy are generally based on the credibility. That is why it is so important to know how you can recognise deep fake and fake news.

Source: Laurens Verhagen, 'Zo maak je een griezelig echte nepvideo', de Volkskrant

DECIDE WHO YOU WANT TO COSPLAY.

Choose a character you can relate to or that you are similar to. Keep in mind that you don't have to cosplay as your race, body type, or gender; anyone can cosplay. On a similar note, your cosplay does not have to be from anime or anything of Japanese origin. You can cosplay a character from a movie, television show, or even a western animation.

'How to Cosplay', with wikiHow Staff

Fake it till you make it is the well-intended and intelligent advice to insecure fumblers, scaredy-cats, wallflowers or introvert, shy characters. As soon as you pretend not to be scared, good, agree, introvert, or inhibited, you will overcome the obstacles of the soul and become what you initially only pretended to be. Faking is the path to a longed-for change in reality. Fake it till you make it recommends deploying the human imagination with the goal of succeeding in life. This brilliance and dangerous ability to pretend forms the core of morality.

Connie Palmen, 'Waarheid is fictie', *Vrij Nederland*

ARE YOU AUTHENTIC?

 YES  NO

MOTIVATE

HOW DO YOU KNOW THAT YOU ARE REAL?

HOW HUMAN DO YOU CONSIDER YOURSELF TO BE?

INHUMAN 1 2 3 4 5 6 7 8 9 10 HUMAN

If you are a non-human life form, what species or type are you?

If known, where were you assembled or born?

IF KNOWN, WHO DESIGNED YOU?

If known, who programmed you?

If known, what is the language of your source code?

If known, under what operating system are you running?

IF KNOWN, ON WHAT HARDWARE ARE YOU RUNNING?

howhumanareyou.com

HOW WILL YOU LIVE ON AFTER DEATH?

DEATH

YOU ARE MAKEABLE, ALSO AFTER DEATH.

YOU PROLONG, REPAIR, DESIGN AND CREATE.

YOU WANT TO BE THERE AS LONG AS YOU CAN.

THE FUTURE AFTER DEATH IS A BUSINESS MODEL.

Mieke Gerritzen

DEAD PEOPLE DON'T CONSUME.

HOW WILL YOU LIVE ON DIGITALLY AFTER YOU'VE DIED?

AS A TREE?

According to the late Apple founder Steve Jobs, death is the best invention life ever made.

> # By burying the old we clear the way for something new. That is a creative mechanism invented by evolution in order to renew itself.
>
> Steve Jobs

DEATH IS A DESIGN ISSUE.

In theory, design could — and should — have a useful part to play in improving the quality of any aspect of daily life that is no longer fit for purpose, and death is no exception.

Alice Rawsthorn in 'Reinventing Death for the Twenty-first Century', designcouncil.org.uk

WOULD YOU LIKE TO CONTINUE LIVING TOGETHER AFTER YOU'VE DIED?

☐ YES ☐ NO

MOTIVATE _____

The death of a loved one is always a sad affair. However, in the future you may be able to stay in contact through a simulation that is so lifelike that you hardly notice the difference. Imagine what it would be like if you never really would have to say goodbye to anyone anymore (until you yourself die). 'What counts, is that the simulation "feels real", that it provides an emotional connection that softens the pain of the loss and allows for a new form of closure.'

'Death-tech en de toekomst van de dood', richardvanhooijdonk.co

Stefan Schafer, *Digital Death and the Post-Mortem Self*, 2015

Each selfie is a flirtation with death; each selfie is an expression of romance and deep down it is melancholic as it attempts to grab something that is intangible. Photography makes this possible: even the image betrays us. And we surrender without a struggle. We don't know any better. Also not on holidays when we fill our cameras with snapshots. Actually, all words, all images are a holiday from reality, a small goodbye, a marking of time, a moment of quiet bordering on silence, on emptiness, on the void. The whiteness of death.

Yra van Dijk, Leegte, *leegte die ademt*

WHEN WILL YOU DIE?

Descartes described our body as a machine that is brought to life by a soul created by God in the pineal gland of the brain. Later, Dr Duncan McDougall maintained that the soul was an object that had mass. He attempted to prove this in a study in which he weighed patients just before and immediately after death. Now, some hundred years later, we know that life is not surrounded by some magical substance. Still, we do not know everything yet.

Anne Dumoulin, 'Wanneer ben je dood?', deeconometrist.n

DO YOU DESIGN YOUR OWN DEATH?

☐ **YES** ☐ **NO**

MOTIVATE _____

HOW WILL YOU DIE?

Euthanasia advocate Philip Nitschke has created a 3D-printed suicide machine (Death Pod) that allows users to administer their own death in a matter of minutes. By pressing a button on the inside of the pod the machine floods with liquid nitrogen, an unregulated substance that can be easily purchased. When you're ready you say goodbye, use the code to get in, pull down the canopy, press a button and you die in a few minutes. Source: Gunseli Yalcinkaya, 'Philip Nitschke's 3D-printed "death pod" lets users die at the press of a button', dezeen.com

Paola Antonelli, design curator in New York, advocates that if mankind becomes extinct, we should design our end elegantly so that the future will look back with respect on the phenomenon of human beings.

Source: Suzanne Labarre, 'MoMA Curator: "[Humanity] Will Become Extinct. We Need to Design an Elegant Ending', fastcompany.com

DESIGN YOUR OWN DEATH

In 10 years

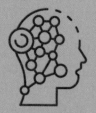
In 100 years

In 1000 years

In 10,000 years

DEATH EVOLVES WITH MANKIND

We can talk about death; it may even be a romantic part of our lives.

IS YOUR DEATH A CREATIVE ELEMENT FOR YOU?

 YES NO

MOTIVATE _____

WHICH TREE WOULD YOU LIKE TO BE AFTER DEATH?

Ashes are held in an egg-shaped pod that is then buried as a seed in the earth, capsulamundi.it

DRAW THE TREE YOU WANT TO BECOME.

LEAVE
COMMENTS,
MESSAGES
OR IDEAS!

SELFDESIGN.NL